Beggars & Builders

My Story of Gorton Monastery

Monastery Publications

Assisi to Gorton
by Fr. Agnellus Andrew

Gorton Monastery, 1861 – 1961
By Fr. Justin McLoughlin

The Greyfriars Players, 1937 – 1948
by Fr. Agnellus Andrew

The Return of the Saints
by Janet Wallwork

Beggars & Builders

My Story of Gorton Monastery

By

Tony Hurley

Edited by Janet Wallwork and Ray Hanks

Second Edition

Monastery Publications

Beggars and Builders: My Story of Gorton Monastery
By Tony Hurley
First published by The Monastery of St Francis and Gorton
Trust, Manchester, in 2011.
Second Edition, 2013.

ISBN 978-0-9571484-0-6

Printed in Great Britain by Book Printing UK, Remus House,
Coltsfoot Drive, Woodston, Peterborough PE2 9BF

Cover design by **Imagine**: Graphic Designers, The Stables, Paradise Wharf,
Ducie Street, Manchester M1 2JN

All proceeds from the sale of this book will go to
The Monastery of St Francis and Gorton Trust,
Gorton Lane, Manchester, M12 5WF
Registered Charity No. 1061457

THE
MONASTERY
OF ST FRANCIS & GORTON
TRUST

www.themonastery.co.uk

Dedication

To my brother

Brendan Hurley

&

To Life Itself

Contents

Foreword

It was in 1998 at a Heritage Conference in Manchester Town Hall when I was introduced to Tony Hurley. At that time we were in the early days of the Monastery Trust. It was a struggle to raise funds and to generate the support we needed to try to save Gorton Monastery. The buildings were in a derelict and sorry state and I desperately needed all the support I could get to help the campaign.

Tony knew the Monastery and immediately offered to support us in whatever way he could. At the time he was Business Development Director at the environmental charity, Groundwork Manchester, and he very kindly brought an army of unemployed young people to help us tidy up the site and keep the gardens under control. It didn't take long for the Monastery to get under Tony's skin in the way that it seems to with everyone who spends time here.

Over the years Tony spent more and more time helping with ideas, writing and advising on bid documents and explaining to me all the different varieties of hawks and species of urban wildlife, telling me fascinating facts about their habits and behaviour that he had observed as they inhabited the rambling dereliction of our Monastery site.

It wasn't long before we invited Tony to join our board of trustees. His wide range of skills and talents were a huge asset to the Trust and his love and support for the Monastery was plain to see. Tony and I worked closely together for 10 years and he was always at the end of the phone with his wise words of encouragement and his common sense advice, that helped to keep me grounded and motivated when the going got tough.

Of course, those years were a very challenging time for all of us and we seemed to take it in turns to prop each other up emotionally, financially and practically when we seemed to be facing insurmountable problems with our crumbling building and the constant frustrations around the bids process.

Our original little team of Audrey, Ailsa, Ilma, Iram, David, Kath, Tony and myself just about managed to hold it together until our fortunes changed and the funding was finally approved for restoration to begin in 2005.

That was when Tony really came into his own. He was a quiet, unassuming man who would never put himself in the limelight but the opportunity to tell the Monastery story seemed to transform him. In those days we organized "hard hat" tours from the Angels community building, just across the road from the Monastery. The minute Tony put on his "high vis" jacket and gathered his groups of visitors around him, a remarkable transformation seemed to take place. Not only did his immense knowledge of the building shine through, but his eyes used to sparkle with the stories of the Franciscan brothers as if he had actually been there with them and he was *reminiscing* rather than telling someone else's story.

In the years that followed "Tony's Tours" became famous. He was always uncovering more facts and figures with his endless research into the history, the hidden secrets of the building and the Franciscans' story. Every tour was informative, inspiring, and often moved our visitors, and ourselves, to tears.

Of course, with all things in life we tend to assume they will always be there. It was like that with the Monastery, which was nearly lost forever, and it was the same with Tony. We always assumed that Tony would be there with his immense knowledge and incredible memory to call on every time we needed that special piece of information. Nothing was ever too much trouble for Tony when visitors turned up at the Monastery. He would welcome weary travellers, research their family history, make all of our visitors welcome and he provided genuine Franciscan care, compassion and hospitality to everyone.

Tony was wonderful with the older generation and he had such genuine interest in their personal stories. I learned so much from him in so many ways.

Tony's illness took a hold in late 2010 and his condition deteriorated rapidly. Amazingly, despite his constant pain and the freezing December weather, Tony insisted on carrying out his Christmas Tours from his wheelchair, right up to the very end.

Thankfully for all of us, Tony lives on in this book. This story is his legacy and we are so thrilled that we can make it available to everyone so soon after this very important year, 2011. Not only is it published in loving memory of our dear friend Tony but it is also to commemorate the 150th Anniversary of the Franciscans' arrival here in Gorton. Tony would have wanted that. He also wanted to see the Saints returned safely to the Monastery in this important anniversary year and we are also delighted that we have been able to achieve that too, even though we are still in the process of raising funds for their restoration.

When you read the book I am sure you will get a feeling for Tony's warmth and personality as it shines through in his unique style and sense of humour. I am greatly honoured to write this foreword for Tony's book. More importantly, I know

I have been blessed to know such a wonderful man and to have had the privilege of sharing his company and his friendship for such a major part of both our lives.

It has been a revelation on many levels. I miss Tony so much although many of us still sense his presence around the Monastery. I am so grateful for the memories and for Tony being my right hand man for so long.

I am indebted to all those who have helped to get this important book published, particularly two of the Monastery Trustees, Janet Wallwork and Ray Hanks. Janet had previously helped Tony with some of the research for the book, and so, together with Ray, was able to complete and edit Tony's final draft, to ready it for publication. I know that Tony would be thrilled that others can now share his story and understand the hidden secrets of Gorton Monastery.

Tony's book has inspired us to initiate a new venture – Monastery Publications. This book is the first of a series that will include both new works, and reprints of previously unavailable texts. We hope to carry on Tony's mission to discover and share the wonderful history of the Monastery, and of the surrounding area.

Elaine Griffiths, MBE
Chief Executive
The Monastery of St Francis and Gorton Trust
December 2011

Editors' Preface

This book represents the fruition of over seven years of work by our dear friend, Tony Hurley. It is fortunate that, at the time of his premature death, the majority of the text had actually been completed. It has been our pleasure and our privilege to ready his final draft for publication. We have noted his few omissions, and provided footnotes in those places we felt necessary, in the interests of clarity. Some minor corrections were made to spelling and grammar.

One difficulty we faced was identifying the illustrations which Tony wished to use in the book, and obtaining good quality reproductions of these. Some older photographs proved challenging, but we have used all means possible to restore and enhance the images he chose. One task Tony was unable to finish was obtaining permission from the copyright holders for the use of quotations and illustrations. We have made every effort to trace the rights holders and to obtain their permission for the use of copyright material. We apologise for any errors or omissions in the acknowledgments and credits, and would be grateful if notified of any corrections that should be incorporated in future reprints or editions of this book.

Acknowledgements

Anyone who reads this book will realise that Tony's researches enjoyed the wholehearted support of all those connected with the Gorton Monastery project, as well as many people, far and wide, whose paths he crossed. His enthusiasm and dogged determination to uncover the Monastery's story, which shine throughout the pages of this book, help to explain some of the support he attracted from those with whom he made contact. We sincerely regret that we are not able to name all those whose help we are sure that Tony would have acknowledged.

We do know he would have thanked the Minister Provincial of the Franciscan Order of Great Britain (O.F.M.) for generously allowing him to use the quotations and illustrations from original publications they produced about the Monastery, and Sotheby's for the use of their photographs of the Saints' statues. Aileen Lawrence and Judy Buller were amongst many people who helped with his research. Graham North, the Monastery's excellent and indefatigable photographer provided many images, and Cath Thomson gave the book its final proofreading. David Ratcliffe gave the editors tremendous help with all the technical aspects of bringing this book to press. Clare Mount dealt with the printers and was instrumental in carrying out the necessary revisions and corrections for this Second Edition. We ask forgiveness from anyone we have omitted.

Janet Wallwork and Ray Hanks
Trustees
The Monastery of St Francis and Gorton Trust
December 2011

Photo credits
The Franciscan Order of Great Britain (O.F.M.):pp 22, 29, 41, 47, 93, 96, 98 (2), 100, 110, 155, 164.
Tony Hurley: pp 58, 64, 65, 88, 92, 107, 116 (3), 130, 135, 136, 140, 142, 148, 153.
Aileen Lawrence: p104.
Alison Levesley: p143.
Graham North: pp 24, 48, 69, 72, 73, 75, 76, 77, 78, 83, 128, 131, 132, 144 (2), 163.
A private collection: p 21.
Sotheby's: p 60 (2).

Chapter 1: My Journey

I lived in West Gorton as a teenager in the sixties and have to admit I can't recall the Monastery in any detail. I do remember a large black church on Gorton Lane and the crowds that used to throng the lane on Sunday mornings after mass. I even attended baptisms of my nephew and nieces, although the splendour of the magnificent Pugin architecture was lost on me.

In 1998 I met Elaine Griffiths at a regeneration meeting in Manchester Town Hall, and she told me about the plans to restore Gorton Monastery. At that time, my job involved providing training and employment opportunities for 18-24 year olds as part of a government initiative. I had also made three successful lottery bids and had secured numerous European funding packages. This knowledge and these skills were obviously of great benefit to the Monastery, and I began volunteering with Elaine and others. In time, I was asked to join the Monastery as a trustee and, in 2005, was employed as a project manager by The Monastery of St Francis and Gorton Trust.

In 1938 a booklet was published by Fr. Agnellus Andrew, 'Assisi to Gorton', to celebrate the consecration of the church and giving its history from 1861.[1] In 1961 Fr. Justin McLoughlin published another booklet, 'Gorton Monastery 1861-1961', to celebrate the centenary of the Franciscans'

---

[1] Andrew, Fr. Agnellus (1938) *Assisi to Gorton... A brief record of the work of the Franciscans in England, and especially of their work at Gorton, 1861-1938.* Buckingham: E.N.Hillier. This was reprinted in 2012 by Monastery Publications, Manchester.

arrival in Gorton.[2] Both booklets provided a wealth of information on the history of the Monastery but it was much later that I discovered that only part of the story of Gorton Monastery had been told. There was an even more fascinating history that had been long forgotten, and which began to unfold as I started to research the history of the Monastery.

My journey of discovery was twofold, encompassing both the history of the Monastery and my own spiritual growth. It began in February 2005 when I was in the Monastery with some students who were making a short film as part of their coursework. I was there to ensure the safety of the students and, for once, was able to just lean against one of the columns and enjoy the beautiful silver sunshine streaming through the windows. As the morning progressed, I noticed that the lights from the clerestory windows were tracking across the wall as the sun rose, and would shortly illuminate significant parts of the nave. More of this later but I was so astonished by what I saw, that it led me to research more into the history of the Monastery and, in particular, the friars who had achieved so much.

One question I am often asked is about the name 'Gorton Monastery', when actually the buildings are The Church of St. Francis and The Friary of St. Francis. The simple explanation is that monks live in a monastery and stay in the monastery and devote themselves to God. Friars, on the other hand, live in a friary and work out in the community with the poor and needy. No doubt the Franciscan brothers explained the difference to the Victorian working classes but the explanation went in one ear and out the other. "You act like a monk, you dress like a

---

[2] McLoughlin, Justin (1961) *Gorton Monastery: story of 100 years of the Friary, Gorton, Manchester*. Eccles: J.E.Mulligan & Co. This was reprinted by Monastery Publications, Manchester, in 2012.

monk, so this must be a monastery" and the name has stuck ever since, even though it says 'St. Francis Friary' on the garden gate.

The title of this book 'Beggars and Builders: My Story of Gorton Monastery', was inspired by an internal memo to the Board of Education in Whitehall dated 27th November 1915. The civil servant begins the memo with *'I should like to take the Board's opinion on a rather delicate matter of procedure'* and then goes onto explain that the boys' school at Gorton is on the Black List because of cramped and overcrowded conditions. Because of the war effort, no public funding was available towards improvements but the civil servant had been approached by the new Superior of the Monastery, who wanted to carry out the improvements without Board of Education funding. He goes on to explain, *'As it happens, however, a new Superior has taken charge of the Franciscan Monastery and he is eager to begin to plan for new schools. He is one of the seasoned 'beggars and builders'. He says that his people are now making much money (Gorton being a considerable munitions industry area) and like the Treasury, he wishes to tap it.'* 'Beggars and builders' conjured up such a vivid picture of the friars I have come to love, that it seemed a most appropriate title for this book. The subtitle had originally been *'The' Story of Gorton Monastery.* With hindsight, however, it is *'My'* story, as all those who have been involved with the Monastery have a different story to tell.

Chapter 2: Gorton 1861

In the last days of November 1861, three Belgian Franciscan Fathers and one Irish Franciscan Brother arrived in Gorton by train to establish the Parish of Gorton. The site where Gorton Monastery was to be built was, at that time, Bankfield Cottage, surrounded by four and a half acres of land. On their first visit, the Franciscans would have noted that the cottage stood off Gorton Old Road, which was then lined with mature Poplar trees. Opposite the cottage was a pond with ducks and geese and behind that was Warburton Farm. Journeying past Warburton Farm, you would go through Pasture Field, then Strawberry Field, and arrive at Belle Vue Gardens less than half a mile away. Belle Vue was maturing from tea gardens but was yet to become a world famous amusement park and zoo.

Looking south east from Bankfield Cottage, the Franciscans would have seen the town of Gorton, which numbered about 3,000 people, mainly engaged in agriculture, cotton and the emerging engineering industries. North east from the cottage, Gorton Tank and Bayer Peacock were steadily growing and would produce over 8,000 steam engines in the next 100 years. The industry had been attracted to the area by the availability of coal from collieries in nearby Bradford, and steel from the works on Bessemer Street. Lower rates in Gorton than in Manchester would have provided a financial incentive but of paramount importance was the fact that this area was the first flat ground to be found on the route of the Sheffield, Ashton and Manchester Railway. The line coming out of Manchester is carried on a viaduct, until it arrives just north of Bankfield Cottage. This is the first opportunity to turn a locomotive on or off the track and was the reason for Gorton Tank and Bayer Peacock locating in Gorton. Bankfield Cottage is located at the top of the hill leaving Manchester, which has some significance to our story.

Whilst we know that the Franciscans took up residence in Bankfield Cottage on 25th April 1862, it is not clear whether or not they knew of the cottage when they took their journey to Gorton in the last days of November 1861. The Belgian Province had been negotiating with Bishop Turner of Salford since 1856, and a now unknown location was identified as early as 1857. Fr. Emmanuel Kenners had visited Manchester from Sclerder in September. Given that they were going to stay with Fr. Cardinael (a fellow Belgian) in nearby St. Ann's Church, Fairfield and that Fr. Cardinael had just completed the building of St Patrick's Boys' school adjacent to Bankfield, it is more than likely that they would have known of its existence. I can, therefore, imagine the excitement of the three Belgian Franciscan priests and the young Irish Franciscan Brother viewing the site from the train from Manchester.

A view of Manchester in 1844

19

Looking west from Bankfield Cottage, the land slopes gently down through farms and fields, past the township of Ardwick and crosses the R. Medlock, climbing again to reach Manchester about three miles away. Manchester had become a city just eight years earlier, and its post industrial revolution townscape was characterised by the mill buildings and chimneys, surrounded by dense poor quality housing in which 300,000 people worked and lived.

In 1862 the mill chimneys would be strangely idle, as the American Civil War had begun the previous April. Whilst the blockade of Confederate ports was not yet effective, the mill owners were stockpiling their cotton and waiting for the price to increase; in the meantime, people were being laid off work and we were at the very beginning of the 'cotton famine'. During the next four years at the height of the famine, up to 400 people a day would receive food from the friary.

Fr. Germain blessed the chapel in St Patrick's school and said the first mass there on Christmas Day in 1861. Exactly four months later, the Franciscans took up residence in Bankfield Cottage and prepared to build their new church. The Franciscans had been granted the Parish of Gorton by the Rt. Rev. William Turner, Bishop of Salford. The parish in those days covered Gorton and parts of Bradford, Openshaw, Fairfield, Longsight and Reddish; an area of approximately 25 square miles and containing about 300 Catholics.

The Franciscans, despite having little money because of their vow of poverty, engaged the services of Edward Welby Pugin as architect.

Together with the Franciscans, Edward, the son of Augustus Welby Pugin, who designed much of the Houses of Parliament, came up with a plan to build a Parish church of cathedral-like proportions to meet the needs of just 300 Catholics spread over 25 square miles.

Edward Welby Pugin

Towering forty feet higher than Manchester Cathedral, six feet higher than York Minster and within four feet of Westminster Abbey, the church of St. Francis can lay just claim to cathedral-like proportions, at least in height if not in length.

Intriguingly, despite Edward Pugin's description of the church he was going to build, in the architectural journal *The Builder*, as being orientated east-west, as is traditional in most religions, the church is built on a north-south orientation. Whilst the orientation of churches is often dependent on the shape of the site, there was certainly enough room in Bankfield to have laid out the church in the traditional manner. There was a growing tendency for the so called 'industrial churches', built to hold large congregations gathering in the growing cities, to be built with the doors on the main thoroughfare. There may, however, be a more compelling reason for building the church of St. Francis on a north-south alignment.

So why would the poor Franciscans, famed for their humility, build a 'cathedral' for a parish church and why on that unusual alignment? To understand part of the reason, it is necessary to look at the history of the Franciscans in England.

Chapter 3: Giovanni di Bernadone

God's Troubadour

St. Francis, from a Stained glass window above the High Altar.

Much has been written about St. Francis and he is perhaps one of the best loved Saints. Born Giovanni (John) di Bernadone, in Assisi, he was nicknamed Francesco (little Frenchman) by his father. I have thought long and hard about this chapter and how much to write about the life of St. Francis, which would be a book in itself. In order for you to understand Gorton Monastery, I have decided to use Fr. Agnellus Andrew's description from 'Assisi to Gorton' published in June 1938, as it eloquently expresses both the story of St.

Francis and Fr. Agnellus' love of him, and the essence of being a Franciscan.

'Arise, Francis, and restore my house for it is falling into ruins.' Francis laboured with stone and mortar in literal obedience to the voice which spoke to him from the Crucifix. First he rebuilt St Damian's, then St Peter's and then St Mary of the Angels which later he loved so much – his Portiuncula. He did not know that he had been chosen by God to be the Father of many sons, who, wearing his habit and bearing his name, would labour for God and his Church in every country of the world.

The Order was born on a winter's day of 1209 when Francis in St. Mary of the Angels heard the priest read in the Mass of how Christ sent forth his disciples: And going to preach, saying; "the Kingdom of Heaven is at hand. Heal the sick, raise the dead. Cleanse the lepers, cast out devils. Freely have you received; freely give. Do not possess gold nor silver nor money in your purse. Nor scrip for your journey nor two coats, nor shoes, nor a staff." Here was clear cut guidance. Here was unmistakable direction. From now on this was to be his life. Later when others came to join him they must do as he did, and when he came at last to write the Rule for his Order he began with these words: 'To observe the Gospel of Our Lord Jesus Christ.' Disciples came rapidly and soon Francis was one of a great number of poor men of Assisi. Bernard of Quintavalle was the first, a prominent man in the town whose coming caused a sensation; then Pater Catani, a lawyer; then Guy, then a whole host of others. When there were still but twelve of them Francis decided he must see the Pope to get his approval, and off they went together to Rome. At first it seemed as though their visit was to be in vain but in the end Innocent III relented and gave his oral approval to the Rule, moved by the advice of Cardinal John of St. Paul, and moved, too, by a vision that he had by night in which he saw this poor little ragged man

25

steadying and supporting his great Basilica of St. John Lateran which was tottering as though to fall. Later in 1215 the Order was recognized by the IVth Council of the Lateran, and the Rule was finally approved by a Bull of Pope Honorius III in 1223. So began the Order of Friars Minor.

Those early days were full of beauty. Read Thomas of Celano's 'Lives of St. Francis,' read the 'Fioretti,' or the 'Mirror of Perfection,' or the 'Legend of the Three Companions' and you will understand why the world loved the friars, and why the family of Francis grew till he numbered thousands of his children. They were first and foremost, men of God, aflame with a seraphic love and detached from things of this world, and their mission was to communicate this divine fire to those around. They were not merely preachers. They were men of God bringing God to the people, and weaning them from the evils of the world, by their example as by their word. Preaching to them, working among them, praying always. They did not idle their time away. Francis wished for no Brother Fly among the brethren. They were to work, and teach, and preach, but always in such a way that 'they do not extinguish the spirit of holy prayer and devotion to which all created things is meant to contribute.' They were poor and needy. Had not their Father espoused Lady Poverty? Yet they were not censorious of others: 'Let all the brethren be clad in poor garments, and they may patch them with sackcloth and with other pieces with the blessing of God. I warn and exhort them not to despise or to judge those whom they see clad in apparel soft and coloured, and using choice foods and drinks; but rather let each one judge and despise himself - Let the brethren appropriate nothing to themselves, neither house nor land nor anything, and as pilgrims and strangers in this world, serving the Lord in poverty and humility let them go confidently for alms: and they should not be ashamed of this because the Lord made Himself poor in this world for us. This is the summit of highest poverty which constitutes you my dearest brothers, heirs and princes of the Kingdom of Heaven: which has made you poor in earthly things, but raised you up in virtue. Let this be your portion leading into the land of the living. Dearest brethren, clinging wholly to this may you never wish to have aught else here below in memory of Our Lord Jesus Christ. Wherever the brethren are and meet together let them show that they are members of the same family, and frankly expose their needs one to another, for if a mother loves and cherishes the son that is born to her, how much more should each one love and cherish his spiritual brother: and if anyone should fall ill, the other brethren ought to serve him as they wish to be served themselves.'

Wherever they went they strove for the reformation of the people, preaching Christ and Him crucified, preaching penance, preaching the gospel that they were trying to live. Italy, Spain, Germany, Morocco, Syria, France and England heard their voice before the death of Francis, and within thirty years of his death, the Franciscans had penetrated even to Japan, and China and Mongolia. Many are the stories of the exploits of those early missionaries, such as the story of the friars who first went to Germany. They knew but one word of German, 'Ja,' which means 'yes,' and they answered this to every question, even when they were asked if they were heretics or infidels. Small wonder that they were sometimes badly received and roughly treated, these strange looking men, with their strange, coarse ragged habit and cord and their bare feet. It did not take long for them to win the heart of the people, and there was no more familiar and no better loved figure in medieval Europe than the friar of St. Francis.

St. Bonaventure carried the habit of Francis into the Councils of the church: St. Bernardine and many carried it to the mission fields of Italy: St. John Capistran made it glorious in the Crusades: John Duns Scotus and his followers made it known in the University Halls of England and France and Germany. Four popes have worn their Franciscan habit beneath their papal robes, as have many hundreds of cardinals and bishops in every land of the world. But the most glorious page in Franciscan history is the one which tells of those who have died for Christ, from those first Troubadours of god who died joyously in Morocco 700 years ago, to those gallant and brave men who died in Spain but yesterday. (A reference to the 44 Franciscans who were martyred in the Spanish Civil War) Filii Sanctorum Sumus. (We are children of saints).

Fr. Agnellus Andrew

Many people who come on tours of Gorton Monastery ask me if I know of Fr. Agnellus Andrew. He certainly seems to have made an impression on people and is remembered for his humour. Fr. Agnellus (Mathew) Andrew was born in Crosshill, Ireland on the 27th May 1908 and ordained as a priest in the Order of Friars Minor on the 20th February 1932. He founded and led the Greyfriars Operatic Group at Gorton Monastery, whose performances of Gilbert & Sullivan were legendary. As Fr. Justin was later to write, the Greyfriars and Parochial Choir under Fr. Lawrence Powell and Fr. Agnellus Andrew attained a standard unique in the city. The Halle Chorus was willing to join it, the BBC pursued it, and the dramatic and operatic level in Gorton Parish was recognised throughout the city as being uncommonly high. During WWII, Fr. Agnellus took his Greyfriars Players to Air Force camps and Army centres to produce one 'Gilbert & Sullivan' after another, The Mikado alone being requested all over the Manchester area. [3]

---

[3] The book which Fr. Agnellus wrote about the Players in 1948, *The Greyfriars Players Book, 1937-48*, Openshaw: Mark Hughes, has been reprinted by Monastery Publications, Manchester in 2012.

He was a skilled communicator and, as a member of the Gorton community, had already represented the Church in the radio programme known as the 'The Anvil' (similar to the Brains Trust) and many more 'Brains Trusts'[4] were brought to Gorton, involving Lord Pakenham, the Countess of Listowel, Richard Stokes, Dr. Heenan and Quentin Hogg.

Following his appointment as Catholic Correspondent for the BBC, he was made Vice President of the Pontifical Commission of Social Communications in Rome, and was ordained Bishop in 1980.

Fr. Agnellus pictured, centre, at one of the Greyfriars productions.

---

[4] The 'Brains Trust' started on BBC Radio in 1941, developing into one of the most popular programmes ever broadcast. [Eds.]

Today The Bishop Agnellus Andrew (BAA) Scholarship Fund is an outreach of the Catholic Academy for Communication Arts Professionals, with the purpose of ensuring that minority students from the USA, Canada, and students from developing nations, have access to training for, and a voice in shaping, future communications efforts in the Catholic Church. It was established in 1989 to honour the memory of the late Bishop Agnellus Andrew, OFM, who founded the Catholic Radio and Television Centre in Hatch End, England.

My fondest story about Fr. Agnellus comes from his days at the BBC. While serving as the BBC's adviser on Roman Catholic affairs, Fr. Agnellus received a letter one day from a producer, asking how he might ascertain the official Roman Catholic view of heaven and hell. Fr. Agnellus answered him in a memorandum comprising a single word: 'Die'.

Chapter 4: The First English Province

On the 10th September 1224, nine Franciscan friars landed at Dover and made their way to Canterbury. The leader of the friars was Agnellus of Pisa, a disciple and friend of St. Francis. Having established the Order in Paris, he returned to Italy to attend the Chapter of Mats in 1221, and was sent by St. Francis to found the Order in England.

On arrival at Dover they had been taken for spies, despite having three English friars in their party, and were only allowed to go when one of the friars took off his cord and jokingly offered it to the people to hang them with.

From Canterbury the friars travelled to London and then onto Oxford. Within seven weeks, friaries had been established in these cities, and within a few years friaries had been established in Reading, Northampton, Worcester and Hereford. By the middle of the 13th century, there was hardly an important town in England that didn't have a friary.

Because of their work with the poor and needy, their academic prowess in theological matters, and their lack of materialism and political ambition, they were probably the most powerful religious influence on the religious life of England for the next 300 years. By the 1530s, approximately 1,700 friars were living in 60 friaries throughout Britain. The Franciscans had also established a friary at Greenwich, adjacent to the royal palace, and were effectively chaplains to the royal family. This closeness to the royal family and their profound belief in their Catholic faith ultimately led to the closure of the first English Province, established by Agnellus of Pisa.

In 1534, Frs. Peto and Elstow had been reprimanded for speaking against King Henry VIII's divorce in the presence of the King at the Friary Church in Greenwich. In the same year, Fr. Hugh Rich and Fr. Richard Risby were executed with the Maid of Kent and four priests. In the next few years, more Franciscans suffered death or execution. In 1537 Fr. Anthony Brookley, broken by torture, was strangled with his own cord. In 1538 Fr. Thomas Cort died in neglect in Newgate jail, and Fr. Thomas Belchiam was starved to death for denouncing in writing Henry's claim to be the Head of the Church.

Perhaps the greatest of all those early Franciscan martyrs was Blessed John Forest, the confessor of Queen Catherine of Aragon (herself a Franciscan Tertiary) and the Guardian of the Friary in Greenwich. On 8th April 1538, the holy friar was taken to Lambeth, where, before Cranmer, he was required to make an act of abjuration. This, however, he firmly refused to do, and it was then decided that the sentence of death should be carried out. On 22nd May following, he was taken to Smithfield to be burned. The statue of 'Darvell Gatheren', which had been brought from the church of Llanderfel in Wales, was thrown on the pile of firewood; and thus, according to popular belief, fulfilled an old prophecy that this holy image would set a forest on fire. The holy man's martyrdom lasted two hours, at the end of which the executioners threw him, together with the gibbet on which he hung, into the fire.

By 1540 all the Franciscan friaries had been suppressed by Henry VIII, however the Greenwich friary was revived by Queen Mary, who repaired the buildings and had the friars reinstated on 7th April 1555, by Maurice Griffin, Bishop of Rochester. Reprimanded by the King in 1534, Fr. Peto, now nominally Bishop of Salisbury and soon to be cardinal, and Fr. Elston returned to their old monastery.

They complained to the Queen in July 1555 of having been 'beaten with stones which were flung at them by diverse lewd persons as they passed from London to Greenwich on Sunday last'. The friars were later expelled by Queen Elizabeth on the 12th July 1559, and most of them took refuge in the Netherlands, Lisbon, and in Rome. From 1560 till 1618, there were still Franciscans working in many parts of the country, some being survivors from Queen Mary's time, others having received the habit abroad.

One such friar was Fr. William Stanney who, as the last remaining friar of the first English Province, accepted into the Order John Gennings, who as a result of his brother's martyrdom had converted from Protestantism to Catholicism. Being received into the Church, he entered Douai College, was ordained as a priest in 1607, and was sent upon the English mission the following year. Here he dreamt of the restoration of the English Province of Franciscans, sought out Father William Stanney of the English friars, and from him received the habit, either in 1610 or 1614 (the date is uncertain). After this, he went for a time to a convent of the Order at Ypres, where he was joined by several English companions. From here the foundation of a new English Province was laid, and Father William Stanney recognising the zeal of John Gennings, now gave him the seal of the old Province of the English Franciscans.

Chapter 5: Angelic Battle

Gennings next proceeded to procure a house for the English friars at Gravelines, but in 1618 he obtained leave from the Minister General to establish a settlement at Douai. As a matter of fact, most of the friars who had joined Gennings were alumni of Douai College, and, in transferring their residence to that town, he hoped to obtain a continuous supply of recruits. The work of restoring the English Province was definitely confided to him by the General Chapter of 1618, and he was nominated 'Vicar of England'. To assist him in the work of restoration, the Commissary General of the Belgian nation was empowered to gather together all the English and Scottish friars from any Province in the Order. A decree of the same General Chapter, placed the English Poor Clares of Gravelines under the jurisdiction of English friars. In 1625, the number of the English friars having greatly increased, Gennings sent Fr. Franciscus a Sancta Clara to Rome to plead that the English province be canonically established. The request was granted with the simple restriction that the superior of the province should not assume the title of Provincial, but that of Custos; but in 1629, this restriction was taken away and Friar John Gennings was appointed Minister Provincial. The first Chapter of the new Province was held at Brussels in Advent of the same year, in the convent of the English sisters of the Third Order, which Gennings had himself founded in 1619. This community of tertiary sisters was to play an active role in the events leading to the construction of Gorton Monastery over 240 years later.

From Douai the Franciscans were sent on the English mission, described in Bro. Angelus Mason's book, in 1649, as 'The Seraphic Battle of the Province of England for the Holy

Church of God.'[5] A 'seraphic battle', an 'angelic war' was how they viewed their vocation. Successfully crossing the Channel by night they were less successful in returning and the number of Franciscans executed for the faith since the time of Henry VIII rose still further.

During the religious persecution revived by the Stuart rising in 1745, Fr. Germanus Holmes was seized, consigned by the magistrate to Lancaster Castle and was loaded with iron chains, where for four months he fought the good fight and finished the course of his mortal life, having contracted fever through the filthiness of the place; but not without suspicion of poison administered to him by the wicked woman who brought him his food.

The decline of the Second English Province became noticeable about the year 1770. In assigning the causes, Fr. Thaddeus Herman[6] points to the State laws then enacted against religious communities, which in turn necessarily meant a scarcity of vocations to the Order and a gradual falling off in men and means. In 1773, the French government, in its hostile attitude toward the Church and her institutions, prohibited youths from making religious profession before they had completed their twenty-first year; and, in 1790, another law was passed, pursuant to which no one under French rule was permitted to take vows in a religious order. Douai in Flanders, where the English Franciscans had their novitiate and house of higher studies was, at the time, subject to France, and to their dismay the friars saw how these obnoxious State laws were beginning to affect the Province. By 1790, the Province

---

[5] Actually this was written in Latin: Angelus, a S. Francisco [i.e. Richard Mason] (1649) *Certamen seraphicum provinciæ Angliæ pro sancta Dei ecclesia*, B.Belleri: Douai. [Eds.]

[6] Fr. Thaddeus [i.e.Thaddeus Hermann] (1849) *The History of the Franciscans in England, 1600 -1850*, Art & Book Co.: London.

numbered only forty eight members. Matters came to a head when the French Revolution broke out. On December 19th 1791, the Franciscans were placed under arrest in their house at Douai, and two years later, on 9[th]August, an order was issued by the civil authorities giving the friars one day to leave the town. With a heavy heart, the sixteen resident friars departed for Belgium and took up their abode in a house at Tongres, which the Carmelites generously placed at their disposal; but darker days were yet to come. The triennial chapter of the Province, held in London on 31[st]July 1794, had just made provisions for the house at Tongres when, in the midst of the deliberations, the friars of that place arrived with the sad news that their stay in Belgium was no longer possible. French hordes had invaded the country, and were threatening the lives of priests and religious Orders. The English Franciscans were forced to leave Belgium and return to England. At this time, the Roman Catholic Relief Act 1791 had been passed but it was still an offence to be in a monastic Order.

Now restricted to their mother country, the English Franciscans did all in their power to avert the total extinction of the declining Province. Friends continued to encourage them, by offering material assistance. A novitiate was opened at Osmotherley and later at Aston, although applications for the Order continued to be few and far between. In 1813, the Province numbered only twenty-one members, and in 1838 only nine were left to attend the Chapter held at Clifton. At this Chapter, Fr. Leo Edgeworth was elected Provincial, although, for obvious reasons, the Minister General hesitated to confirm his election and appointed a commissary in the person of Fr. Francis Hendren. Meanwhile, the Sacred Congregation of the Propaganda had taken the matter in hand and, in January 1841, Rt. Rev. Thomas Joseph Brown O.S B., Vicar Apostolic of the Welsh district, notified the Franciscans that the Holy Father had appointed him their Visitor Apostolic. With this provision the English friars, whilst still maintaining a small presence in England, had ceased to exist as a Province.

Chapter 6: The Pioneers

By 1848 there were just four Franciscans left in England, Bishop Francis Hendren at Nottingham, Fr. Bonaventure Fisher at Llanarth in Monmouthshire, Fr. Anselm Millward living in retirement near Leamington, and Fr. Paschal O'Farrell at Weston-super-Mare.

At this point Mother Agnes Jerningham, Abbess of Taunton Convent, lent a hand. Mother Agnes was from the Franciscan Order established by Fr. Gennings in Brussels in 1619. Knowing that the Rt. Rev. Cornelius Von Bommel, Bishop of Liege, was to attend the consecration of the cathedral of St. George, Southwark, and that he was fond of the Franciscan friars in his native Belgium, she invited him to Taunton.

At this point I'll let Fr. Thaddeus Hermann take up the story, with his evocative description of the events of that visit in the summer of 1848[7].

It was a fine summer evening in 1848. A carriage drove swiftly through the dusty streets of Taunton, towards the Franciscan Convent, at the far end of the town.

The visitor was evidently expected, for the Sisters, with the children arranged in due order, had held themselves in readiness for some time, "There he is!" they whispered at last; the door of the carriage was thrown open, and the aged and saintly Bishop of Liege, Cornelius van Bommel stepped out. When the blessing had been given and received in respectful silence, the air rang with joyous peals of welcome.

"My Lord" said the Mother Abbess, "it is extremely kind of you to come to see us, after the long journey you had undertaken to assist at the opening of St. George's Cathedral."

---

[7] Fr. Thaddeus (1869).

The Bishop replied: *"I could not well decline coming to the inauguration of what was once 'the Belgian Chapel.' And, after that, I could not forego the pleasure of coming a little further to see the nuns of the Third Order of the great St. Francis, for whom I have always cherished a special veneration."*

"Half a century has passed, my Lord," explained Mother Abbess, *"since we had to leave your country, where we, as well as our Fathers, had been so hospitably received, and spent many a happy and peaceful day. And now we are doubly glad to welcome you, as the Pastor of the diocese where our fathers found a shelter, when they were expelled from Douai."*

"They would have found a lasting home with us," said the bishop, *"had not the French come to continue in Catholic Belgium, also their disgraceful work of profanation and destruction."*

"Alas! Exclaimed the Abbess," we have lost nearly all our fathers. Scarce half-a-dozen remain: they are getting old, scattered over the country, and there is no hope of their recruiting new members. I wish our Holy Father St. Francis would come to our assistance. But, my Lord, have you any Franciscans in your diocese?"*

"Oh yes!" answered the Prelate,* there are in my diocese three Franciscan friaries, which the Fathers have recovered since the French Revolution. The Franciscans are multiplying rapidly in Belgium, and considering that it is not much more than a dozen years since they were allowed by the law to live in community, their increase is most wonderful."*

"Will your Lordship excuse me," pleaded the Abbess, *'for making so free as to ask what kind of men they are?"*

"They are very exemplary," the Bishop explained, *"and a source of edification to the faithful, and among them many*

learned and holy men. But, Mother Abbess, you ought to know them, for they are the very Fathers that lived side by side with the English Franciscans before the Revolution. When religious Houses were allowed to be reopened, a handful of veterans, who had survived the storms of fifty years, returned to their old homes. I have been told of one of those good old Franciscans, that he was often seen kissing the steps that lead to the choir."

"My Lord!" exclaimed the Abbess, "send us a few of those men."

"Now, Mother Abbess," said the Bishop, "you know that you are asking something which is beyond my power. But for the love of dear St. Francis I promise you that I shall do what I can in the matter. And if I fail to succeed, it will not be my fault."

The Bishop was as good as his word. On his return to Belgium he went straight to the Provincial, and succeeded so well in persuading him, that he lost no time in calling his Definitory together, and laying the matter before them. And they, as zealous children of St. Francis, consented to undertake the arduous task. Ten years, however, were still to elapse before all the arrangements were completed, and the fathers came.

But the record of their labours and vicissitudes must be left to another chronicler.

Sclerder

In fact two more chroniclers take up the story, Fr. Agnellus Andrew in 1938 and Fr. Justin McLoughlin in 1961, both of whose books have provided me with a wealth of information to continue this story.

40

The Pioneers

Left to Right Top: Fr. Francis Verhagen, Fr. Germain Verleyen. Middle: Fr. Archangel Vendrickx, Fr. Emmanuel Kenners, Fr. Patrick Verherstraeten. Bottom: Fr. Bruno De Grave, Fr. Willibrord van der Neucker.

Following the Bishop of Liege's visit, Bishop William Vaughan of Plymouth, wrote to the Belgian Provincial, Fr. Archangel Vendrickx, offering him a house and a church in his diocese. Accompanied by Fr. Emmanuel Kenners, the Provincial set off for Cornwall to inspect the house and church offered to them and approved. On 16th March 1858, the Belgian Province formally accepted this first foundation in England. Fr. Emmanuel returned to Cornwall with Fr. Eustace Princen and immediately set off again for Ireland – to learn English! I find this amazing, particularly as they chose to go to Drogheda to learn English. They spent two months in Drogheda, followed by two and a half years in Cornwall. I can't even begin to imagine what a Belgian, Drogheda and Cornish accent might sound like to the Catholics of Gorton, but nevertheless they managed well enough to be given the Parish of Gorton from the Bishop of Salford.

But for now, back to Cornwall. The Franciscans had been given a small church and house at Sclerder on the Trelawne estate. Lady Anne Trelawney was a Catholic aristocrat who proved to be a generous benefactor to the Franciscans.

Sclerder Abbey, Looe, Cornwall.[8]

[8] From the website of the Parish of Our Lady of the Angels, Saltash (April 2011). Available at http://www.sclerder.talland.org/page2.html . (Accessed 1st December, 2011.) The original source of the drawing is not stated. [Eds.]

Unfortunately, Lady Anne died in July 1860 and was succeeded by a Protestant heir, and all benefactions from the Trelawneys ceased. Finding it impossible to carry on the foundation, it was reluctantly surrendered in 1864.

The first record of Edward Pugin's involvement with the Franciscans is at Sclerder, where he was engaged by them to carry out improvements to the church and house. The 1861 Census shows Fr. Francis Verhagen from Holland to be the head of the household, with Belgians Frs. Emmanuel Kenners, Willibrord van den Neucker and Bruno de Grave with him. Also recorded are two students, Michael Prendergast and Thomas Butti, who later are professed into the Order. Finally, Thomas Bruford and Lambert Heltzer are listed as servants.

During their time in Sclerder, though fairly brief, the Franciscans made over one hundred conversions to Roman Catholicism.

Opening of the Church of St. Francis in Gorton

In 'Gorton Monastery: 1861 – 1961', Fr. Justin tells us;

'The Solemn Opening of the Church took place on 26th September 1872. The Minister General of the whole Franciscan Order, Fr. Bernardine dal Vago a Portugruaro, came from Rome. Archbishop Manning, not yet Cardinal, presided, and also present were Bishop Brown O.S.B, of Wales, Bishop Amherst of Northampton, Bishop Cornthwaite of Beverley, and 250 of the clergy secular and regular. Of the old friars, Fr. Bonaventure Fisher had said his last Mass in April and was not equal to the journey from South Wales, but there on the sanctuary, and on the road to 80, was Fr. Paschal O'Farrell, proudly sporting the new Franciscan habit made especially for the occasion by the Franciscan nuns at Woodchester. In the words of Archbishop Manning, he

represented 'the oldest Franciscan in England, the link which connected the past, present and future of the Franciscan Order in this country'.

And so 26th September 1872 came to a close; a great day for Manchester, for the Minister General of the whole Franciscan Order, for the Provincial of the friars, for Frs. O'Farrell and Fisher, who had worked and prayed for something like this, and could now sing their Nunc Dimittis.[9]

And in 'Assisi to Gorton' Fr. Agnellus quotes the *Catholic Times* of 28th September 1872:

'The Church of St. Francis at West Gorton is a triumph of Catholic Architecture and is many ways a most remarkable work. It is the largest Parish Church built in England since the Reformation.'

From these accounts, we can begin to understand both the cathedral-like proportions of the church and also perhaps the unusual alignment.

If we go back to the 1860s, the site of Gorton Monastery is on the crest of a hill overlooking a river valley, with Manchester on another hill three miles away. In those days, Manchester was a very Protestant city. Not just Protestant but fiercely anti-Catholic; in fact the first Orange Order in England was formed by soldiers returning to the Manchester area from active service in Ireland.

If you could imagine being a Protestant in Manchester at that time, on the skyline three miles away there is a building being

---

[9] Nunc Dimittis.
'Now thou dost dismiss thy servant, O lord, according to thy word in peace;
Because my eyes have seen thy salvation
Which hast prepared before the face of all peoples:
A light to the revelation of the Gentiles and the glory of thy people Israel'

erected broadside onto you. That is the effect of the north south alignment. You would watch in fascination day by day as it rose higher and higher and higher. One awful day, it reaches the height of your Cathedral and doesn't stop! It goes on rising by another forty feet. "What on earth is happening in Gorton?" people would ask. And the answer would be. "Have you not heard? The Catholics are back! Not just the Catholics but those funny Franciscans with the long frocks. And, by the looks of it, they are here to stay this time."

And that is part of the explanation for the amazing height of Gorton Monastery and its unusual alignment. It is an architectural statement in support of a religious belief. After over 320 years of persecution, imprisonment, execution and exile, the Franciscans are making a triumphal return to England. The 'Angelic Battle for the English Province in the Holy Name of God' has begun again.

We no longer have that view of the Monastery because of all the modern buildings in between but if you go up some of the higher buildings in Manchester and look out eastwards, you will see how the Monastery absolutely dominates the landscape.

Building Works at Gorton

I mentioned earlier that three Belgian Franciscan friars and one Irish Franciscan brother arrived in Gorton in December 1861. Why did the Franciscans bring an Irishman with them? It sounds like a stereotype but they would need a builder and he was! Bro. Patrick Dalton, described as being from Kerry or Killarney, certainly looked like a west coast Irishman; big hands, big heart and a big smile.

He was also described as the brick maker, brick carrier, bricklayer, carpenter, joiner, stonemason, sculptor, and clerk of works for the job, and he didn't even get Saturday nights off as he was to be found in the pubs of Manchester and Gorton saying "Let's buy another brick for St Francis." So, he was raising the funds as well.

Bro. Patrick Dalton

Amazingly, within eleven years of his arrival, Bro. Patrick and his Franciscan brothers had built the church and friary themselves. They did not employ builders; they did all the work themselves with the assistance of the 300 Catholics. That is not to say 300 men. Excluding women and children there were perhaps only 30-40 grown men able to help, and then only on evenings and Saturday afternoons.

Even more amazing was that, when digging the foundations, which were up to thirty feet deep and twenty feet wide, Bro. Patrick discovered that, within a foot of the surface, the underlying clay was perfectly good to make the bricks. So Bro. Patrick taught the Catholics how to make timber moulds, smooth out the clay in them, stack them up, build a fire around them and come back at evenings and weekends to help him lay them. If you are handling wet clay, the chances are that occasionally you will leave fingerprints on them and that is exactly what happened. We have evidence of the people leaving finger and thumbprints and even a full palm print! The palm print is so good it was able to be read by a palmist who declared it was somebody about to go on a spiritual journey. Many of the fingerprints seem very small, perhaps suggesting that women and children were engaged in the brick making whilst the men were doing the heavier work.

The Community during the building of the Church.

The figure leaning on the pillar, centre back, is believed to be Edward Welby Pugin.

The following account from *The Harvest* is based on a history of St. Francis published as part of their Golden Jubilee celebrations in 1911.

Year after year they toiled and begged, and at the last after many vicissitudes, a start was made in 1866. We quote the word of the history:-

'Knowing what we do of the enthusiasm of Father Germain and his associates (Father Willibrord, Father Polycarp Vervoort, Father Gommair Peeters, Father Edward Vercoustre, and Father Martin) it is not difficult to realise the excitement that prevailed when the joyous day for actually starting the work of building came around. The news had travelled beyond Gorton. Bishop Turner sent word to say he would come to lay the first stone, and he kept his word. The day chosen was 9th June 1866. An anxious crowd thronged the streets from early morn, and when at last the Bishop began the ceremony of blessing, the grounds were packed with enthusiastic crowds. It was a memorable day - a day that Brother Patrick, the Fathers, and thousands of others ever kept enshrined among their memories of happy days.'

The days succeeding the 9th June were not at all great days. Many a day Brother Patrick and his men were compelled to rest from labour owing to lack of materials and funds. For six months at a time, not a brick was laid. At last in 1871, Fr. Willibrord was appointed Guardian. His appointment was the signal for a mighty effort. No one else seemed to be able to push the work, yet to Fr. Willibrord it appeared to be an easy task. Up and down the country he travelled, always begging and always successful. When the building operations became a charge on him, the magnificent structure had reached but to the height of the nave arches, yet in the space of 18 months Fr. Willibrord completed the work. In the May of 1871 Fr.

Willibrord was appointed Guardian. On 26th September the following year, the church was completed.

The heroes of the day, without a doubt, were Brother Patrick and Father Willibrord. Working hand in hand, they achieved what today would have been nigh impossible. Well might the Fathers and people of Gorton be proud of two such men, Brother Patrick and Father Willibrord, will be remembered in Manchester when all the others are forgotten.

(From *The Harvest* September 1911*).*

Chapter 7: Decline and Dereliction

The following is a re-creation of the newsletter sent to parishioners by Fr. Ronald in 1989, announcing the closure of the church and friary.

5th NOVEMBER 1989 ST. FRANCIS' GORTON TEL. 223.0561

THE THIRTY FIRST SUNDAY IN ORDINARY TIME

My Dear People,

It is with a very heavy heart that I write to tell you all that the day on which the Friars will offer public mass for the last time in our beloved church of St. Francis' Gorton has been decided. It is SUNDAY 26th NOVEMBER. The Feast of Christ the King, just three weeks from today.

I received the news by telephone this morning (Fri. 3rd. Nov.) from Friar Ignatious Kelly O.F.M., our Friar Provincial. The date was chosen during a meeting of our Definitors (the Provincial's Counsellors) held recently. They decided it was kinder to choose and fix a definite departure date rather than prolong the painful suspense any further. While we have been expecting the news, we did not expect to be given such comparatively short notice. We PRESUME that our Definitors again thought it was kinder on us to undergo the painful operation sooner rather than later!

As you will understand during the next three weeks there will be a lot of clearing out, burning, packing and generally finalising all our affairs, to be done. In the circumstances - which will be quite chaotic- we consider it best not to have A SPECIAL LAST MASS with visiting Friars and other clergy, but for the Masses on that week-end to be as usual i.e. the Saturday Vigil Mass at 5.30 pm on the 25th NOVEMBER and the two Masses on Sunday Morning, the 10.15 am being the last Mass. I'm sure you will understand that we won't be in the mood that week-end for presiding over Nostalgic Celebrations!!

There follows some dates and Parish notes and then this final message:

Let's pray for each other!

52

Typing these words today in their beloved Friary nearly 20 years later has been an emotional experience. In recreating Fr. Ronald's words and using his emphasis in underlining and capitals I get a real sense of his anguish.[10]

---

[10] Although Fr. Ronald announced that there would not be a 'special last Mass with visiting friars and other clergy', Bishop Kelly of Salford clearly disagreed. Though there were no visiting friars, the Bishop and his entourage arrived to celebrate the final Mass alongside the resident community, before a church packed to overflowing with a shocked and sorrowful congregation. [Eds.]

A number of factors led to the closure of Gorton Monastery. Firstly, declining church attendance in the 1970s and 80s meant that less money was coming into the church collections, and this led to repairs to the front wing of the friary not being carried out. Secondly, the closure of the engineering industries in Gorton caused massive local unemployment, at a time when national unemployment was already reaching 3 million. This meant there was even less money to spare, and the decision was taken to demolish the front wing of the friary to save money and to provide a car park to alleviate the congestion on Gorton Lane on Sundays.

The final nail in the coffin was the slum clearance, which removed the terraced housing for miles around the Monastery, and resulted in the congregation being dispersed all over Greater Manchester.

Mass was being said for as few as fifty at a time and, in winter, the Franciscans were forced to celebrate mass in the sacristy to save on heating costs. Eventually, the decision was made for the Franciscans to leave Gorton, the building to be sold, and a new smaller Church of St. Francis to be constructed nearby by the Diocese of Salford.

The last mass was said on the 26th November 1989, amongst scenes of great sadness and despair, and the remaining elderly friars left in May 1990.

Father Ronald, the last Guardian (2nd from right) and the remaining friars in the Cloister Garden, in the late 1980s.

Rosa Hugonis

The roses growing over the doorway behind the remaining friars are Rosa Hugonis, named after a Gorton friar. John Aloysius Scallan was born in Rathmines, Dublin, on 6th September 1851, and joined the Franciscan Order as a

55

Novitiate on 30th May 1874 at Thielt in Belgium. He was professed a priest in 1882 and joined the Franciscans at Gorton Monastery in the same year. His post was Assistant Rector of the Seraphic College there, and he left for China in April 1886 to work in the Xian province. In China, Father Hugo discovered a hitherto unknown variety of rose. Rosa Hugonis, sometimes known as the 'Golden Rose of China' or the 'Father Hugo Rose', was introduced in the last century, in 1899. Seed was collected and sent to England from central China by Father Hugh Scallan, a missionary known as 'Father Hugo'. Kew Gardens received the seed, and raised plants from them of this delightful early blooming yellow species rose. Plants of it still thrive there today. During the Boxer Rebellion of 1899 – 1901, which was shortly after his discovery, Father Hugo was beaten unmercifully and almost to death and was, in fact, left for dead. Incredibly, he survived, and finally died some 28 years later on the 6th May 1928, still in China. That's an awful long way from Dublin and Gorton. My beautiful friend Pamela has donated a pair of Rosa Hugonis to replace those lost during the years of dereliction.

Dereliction

Following the Franciscans' departure, the building was sold to a property development company, which immediately sold the Franciscan land to the rear of the property for housing, in order to get back the money that they had paid for the buildings. Anything of value left behind by the Franciscans was taken and sold off for a profit. Planning permission was sought and given for the creation of seven floors of luxury flats in the Church, and more modest flats in the friary. The developer took the deposits for the flats and then went bankrupt, leaving people out of pocket and the building left unguarded.

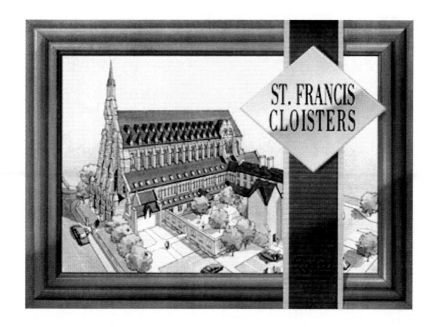

Vandals moved in, and anything of value left by the developer was systematically destroyed. The five magnificent altars were heavily vandalised and every window within a stone's throw, and that was most of them, were broken - allowing water to pour into the building. Thieves stripped the friary of its lead and slates, which again led to severe water damage. Conditions became so bad in the friary that, following heavy thunderstorms in 2004, the floors collapsed right down to the basement in one corner of the friary. At least three fires occurred, gutting the private chapel, the south staircase and part of the friary roof, and the building was left to rack and ruin.

Edward Pugin and Bro. Patrick's 'triumph of Catholic architecture' was left abandoned, derelict and a painful reminder of the high levels of deprivation in Gorton at that time. One thing that did remain, however, was the deep love that those generations of 'Franny' boys and girls had for their beloved Monastery.

Chapter 8: Manchester's Taj Mahal

One such 'Franny' boy was Paul Griffiths, who was an altar boy at the Monastery in the 1960s. He watched the buildings become more and more derelict each time he passed on the train home. Eventually Paul and his wife, Elaine, visited the Monastery, and were able just to push the door open and walk in. Having witnessed the result of years of vandalism and neglect, Paul and Elaine were determined to set up a fund to acquire the buildings and find some way to put them back at the heart of the community.

So determined were they that Elaine gave up her career in marketing to devote herself full time to the task. It is interesting to note that Elaine was awarded an MBE in the 2007 Queen's Birthday Honours; which just goes to show that it took a man to come up with the idea but it took a woman to deliver on it!

The Monastery of St. Francis and Gorton Trust was established in September 1996, and achieved charitable status the following March. The trustees and the Friends of Gorton Monastery began their campaign for support and funding to restore the Monastery, but the main obstacle to securing grant aid was that the Trust did not own the building. This was shortly to change as Gorton Monastery came to the attention of the world.

In 1997, Elaine drew the plight of the Monastery to the attention of the World Monuments Fund (WMF), which is the leading private organisation dedicated to saving the world's most treasured places. Every two years, WMF issues the World Monuments Watch List of 100 Most Endangered Sites, a global call to action on behalf of sites in need of immediate intervention. The initial application was unsuccessful but at the last minute we were included as a result of another site being saved, and so Gorton Monastery crept onto the list in 100th place. Now ranked alongside previous endangered sites like the Taj Mahal and current rankings, including Machu Picchu, Pompeii and the Valley of the Kings, the spotlight of the world fell on Gorton.

Not surprisingly, the press coined the nickname 'Manchester's Taj Mahal' for the Monastery, and suddenly people were taking notice. Along with the WMF listing, came sufficient grant aid to begin the initial feasibility work. The Royal Bank of Scotland were persuaded to sell the Monastery to the Trust for the princely sum of £1, and the battle to secure all the funding needed began in earnest.

Initial approaches to the Heritage Lottery Fund (HLF), supported by English Heritage, were encouraging, and a detailed application was made for the Spirit of Life project. Spirit of Life aimed to provide a centre for the celebration of humanity; providing a venue for people to come to explore issues of life, and share their spiritual and cultural beliefs. Whilst the idea was good, the HLF turned down the application because they felt it would be financially unsustainable.

The Trust managed to find a hotel partner to fund a restoration and extension of the friary into a hotel. The adjoining Church restored with lottery funding would then provide a fabulous venue as part of the complex. Again an HLF bid was submitted, and again it was rejected. This time the HLF thought the scheme to be too commercial, and would raise questions about public funding being used to support the private sector.

Our third and final bid, 'The Pugin Centre', brought together all the best elements of our previous attempts and could be summarised as Corporate, Cultural and Community.

Corporate; providing a venue for businesses and organisations to hold banquets, conferences, award dinners and product launches, as well as providing meeting rooms in the friary.

Cultural; as a large open space, the Monastery is ideal for a wide range of arts events such as drama, dance, exhibitions, choral and music.

Community; putting the building back at the heart of the community with a programme of open days, afternoon tea dances, reminiscence coffee mornings, spiritual and well-being events, but not as a church again - although I will return to this subject later.

This time the application to HLF was successful and we were awarded £3.8 million towards the £5.6 million cost of restoration. One hurdle had been cleared but we still needed to secure another £1.8 million of funding from European Regional Development Funds (ERDF). The complexities of the funding bids involved another year's wait whilst the ERDF funding was secured and, during that time, the costs had escalated to £7 million. We knew that, if we attempted to raise £7 million, the cost would probably rise to £8 million and that, long before we would be able to start work, the buildings would deteriorate to such an extent they would be beyond salvation.

During lengthy negotiations with our funders we carried out a value engineering exercise, taking out of the budget anything that wasn't necessary to have buildings that were restored and habitable, whilst further funding could be found for a second phase. Out went any work to the altars; out went the decorative paint restoration to the chancel; out went the repairs to the chancel floor; out went the landscaping to the garden. Finally, every item in the budget was examined to find the most cost-effective solution until we had balanced the books. In April

2005 we secured the go ahead from our funders to start work; Wm. Anelays Ltd of York was appointed as the restoration contractors and began work on site in November 2005.

This was, arguably, one of the biggest community-led restoration projects to be completed in the country. In total, 300 people took 609 days to restore the grade II* listed building. One hundred miles of scaffolding tubes were erected, enough to stretch end to end from the Monastery to Hadrian's Wall. Amongst the building materials used were 15,000 slate tiles, 125 tonnes of lime mortar and plaster, 400 stained and leaded panes of glass and 20,000 reclaimed bricks.

We had forecast a completion date of 31st March 2007 but we received an unexpected windfall of an additional European grant, which enabled us to install a full banqueting scale kitchen. The further work would take an additional 3 months and, when I heard the new date of completion, it made me curious. I said earlier that Bro. Patrick and his Franciscan brothers had completed their magnificent Church and friary in less than eleven years; in fact the actual time taken was 10 years 9 months and 26 days. Using a date calculator on the internet, it didn't take long to establish that, from the day the Trust was formed to the day we would be given the keys back was 10 years 9 months and 26 days. It had taken us exactly the same length of time to restore the Monastery as it had taken Bro. Patrick to build it!

Chapter 9: Sacred Geometry

'Where there is darkness, light.'

Early in 2005, I received a request from some students to film some short pieces of work in the Monastery for their course exam. It was a frosty day with clear blue skies when they arrived, and I accompanied them to the Monastery and stood around for about half an hour. At that time I would normally be taking people around, walking and talking and not standing still for any length of time. The light coming into the Monastery is absolutely amazing and illuminates the building in most beautiful ways. That day was no exception, and by being still in one place I could watch the sunlight move inch by inch across the walls and floors, as the sun rose higher in the sky. It soon became clear that the lights from the high-up thirteen clerestory windows were tracking across the wall towards the positions where statues of Franciscan saints once stood.

Photos from the Sotheby's sale catalogue, September 1989.

As they inched nearer, it became clear that they would indeed line up. As you can see from the next photo, the lights illuminate the position of each saint and strike the midpoint of the arches in between.

It is an awe-inspiring sight and makes your heart sing. Because of the north south alignment, the whole process takes place again in the afternoon, in reverse, on the opposite wall where the other six saints stood. In the eight years we had owned the Monastery, nobody had actually witnessed this event and, to my knowledge, none of the earlier congregation was aware of it. It happens every day when the sun is shining, occurring earlier or later depending on the time of the year.

As you can see, it's a fabulous spectacle. Notice that the lights match the width and height of the saint and pedestals, despite the clerestory windows (above) being taller and wider.

I can't resist a puzzle and began to wonder about the mathematics and geometry involved to achieve such precision. Also, there are thirteen windows but only twelve 'events' on each wall i.e. saint and arch. Where did the 13th light shine?

Was it to do with Fr. Cuthbert's missing crucifix? Was it perhaps a reference to the twelve Apostles and Jesus Christ?

All twelve of the statues had been recovered in 1994, two years before the Monastery Trust was established. Janet Wallwork, a local resident and historian (who later became a Trustee of the Monastery) spotted an announcement of a forthcoming sale at Sotheby's that showed a photograph of a collection of saints' statues. As a lay member of the Franciscan Community in Gorton she recognised them, and attempted to have the sale halted. After many difficulties, and following six months of negotiations, the City Council stepped in to acquire them in the hope that one day they could be returned to the building. Having spent some time in Manchester Town Hall, the statues are now in a secure container on a Council owned depot with 24 hour security, awaiting restoration.[11]

In the Divine Proportion

So I began looking at the geometry of the church. We have no original plans that show Pugin's geometry. We know that Pugin was using an early 13th century continental gothic style of the type associated with the south of France. Also the floor plan appeared to follow that of a Roman Basilica. Dave Ellis and Melanie Thomas, of Manchester University's Architecture Department, had done survey work earlier and had come up with some interesting theories. I had also tried out various geometries and, between us, there were a number of plausible ways to set out the church; however none of us could satisfactorily explain the little apse that jutted out into the cloister garden.

The apse is an octagonal single-storey feature, that has a quality all of its own. Despite its derelict condition, nearly everyone who visits is drawn to it. In those days, back in 2005, I recognised its beauty and quality, whilst others recognised a spiritual quality or could feel energy in the place. I have since learnt to recognise both its spirituality and its energy.

The apse is the little structure sticking out into the garden and is indicated by an arrow on the following plan. There are a number of odd things about the apse. The cloister garden is rectangular rather than square, and the apse is located off-centre. There is no reason why the apse should be central,

---

[11] In October 2011 the statues were transferred to the Monastery site, in order to undergo restoration. This was completed in June 2012, when the statues were triumphantly returned to their original locations. The full story is told in *The Return of the Saints* by Janet Wallwork: Monastery Publications, 2012. [Eds.]

except you just feel it should be. This, together with its special qualities, led me to take a much closer look at it.

The apse is based on an octagon with 5 sides in the garden and 3 'invisible' sides in the cloister. We didn't know at that time what it was used for as we had no written, oral or photographic record of it.

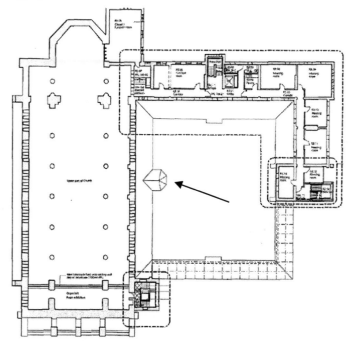

The windows were leaded with a pale green tint (caused by poor quality glass) and gold glass borders. The ceiling was a vivid cardinal red and the floor tiles have a very intricate pattern, different from the cloister and different from the church nave (the bit where people sit). Intriguingly, the only other place to have these tiles is the chancel (the bit where the altar is). My feeling was that, if the chancel is an important place because of the altar, and has those tiles, then perhaps the apse was equally important.

Looking from the outside, its centre seems to be between windows eight and nine of the thirteen clerestory windows at the top of the picture, effectively breaking the clerestory windows into five on the right and eight on the left, and giving us thirteen in all. Suddenly I realised that the sequence 5-8-13 was part of the Fibonacci Series from which we derive the Golden Number, Golden Ratio, the Divine Proportion, and Phi, just to give it some of the many names it has. The Fibonacci Series starts with 0 followed by 1, then you just keeping adding the last to the preceding number to give you the next; 0 1 1 2 3 5 8 13 21 34 55 89 and so on.

To obtain the Divine Proportion you take any number in the sequence and divide it by the previous one, for example $8/5 = 1.6$ and $13/8 = 1.625$.

As you move along the sequence, the number of decimal points gets longer and longer without repeating. In the US they have used super computers to create millions of decimal places and the pattern never repeats. The current accepted shorthand for the Divine Proportion is 1.618. I had come across this about a year earlier and, for some odd reason, I had stored it in my mobile phone and now here was the apse appearing to mark it out on the building. Perhaps the building had a normal section to contain the hoi-polloi, and a Divine Section to contain the first few pews with the great and the good and the clergy and altar. Having established that Pugin appeared to be using the Divine Proportion, I found evidence of it all over the building. My life by then was filled with thousands of calculations, doodles and drawings but I still could not get a satisfactory fit for the apse into the overall geometry of the building

Over time, I returned to the apse and looked at its properties. It is an octagonal design that suggests eight, and eight is the Christian symbol denoting birth, renaissance and regeneration. God created heaven, earth and everything in it, in six days, and on the seventh day, rested. On the eighth is the restart. Start? Well let's start from here. The octagon is twelve feet across and twelve is significant as it often denotes Christ. It also can break down into 1+2=3, denoting the Trinity. The apse has three sides that are invisible and five that are constructed, making eight. Again, 3-5-8 are part of the Fibonacci Series. A feature of an octagon is that every other side but one is at 45 degrees, and that by using two of those sides you can create a 90 degree angle. At last things are starting to make sense! An architect and builder need to create a 90 degree angle when setting out a site. They knock a peg into the ground and set out lines in a fixed direction and length. They also use a technique called 'ad quadratum' by which they set out a square, create a new square on the diagonal, and a third square on the new diagonal. The third square would be twice the size of the first and, by this technique, entire plans could be scaled up from a single square. I incorporated the 'ad quadratum' motif in the landscaping of the garden opposite the apse.

When I applied both the 90 degree and 'ad quadratum' principle to the apse, I found that the apse was used to set up the overall geometry of the church.

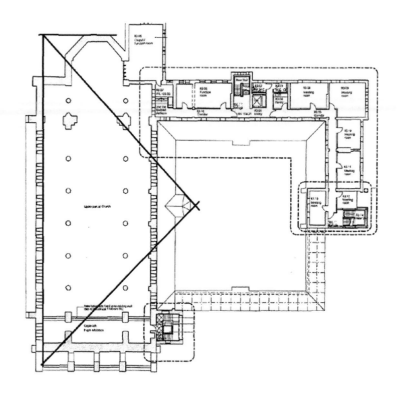

The 90 degree angle gives us a fix on the top of the church and just inside the porch at the bottom of the church, with an exact distance of 84 feet across. Using numerology 84 = 8, 8 + 4 = 12, 1+2=3 giving us the Trinity again. The ad quadratum used on the 12 foot octagon gave us 24 feet and the exact distance to the right hand wall of the church.

I was pleased that I'd discovered that the apse was the architectural heart of the buildings, and that the geometry could be extended to the right to account for the geometry of the friary, but I hadn't explained the proportions within the church to my satisfaction.

Within the church are the nave and the chancel, both beautifully proportioned in themselves and together. The proportion of the nave is quite easy as it is 60 feet wide and 120 feet long, therefore twice as long as it is wide. This is a traditional basilica layout and the diagonal is proportional to the square root of 5 – a classic architectural proportion found in King Solomon's Temple and other holy places. Most people find this the most attractive of all rectangles.

The maths is quite simple if you reduce the dimensions. Effectively it has sides of 1 and 2. Pythagoras Theorem states that the square of the hypotenuse (diagonal) will be the sum of the squares of the other two sides, giving us:

$1^2 = 1$ and $2^2 = 4$ and $1+4 = 5$

So the diagonal is equal to the square root of 5.

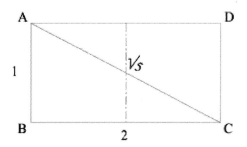

So far so good, but the challenge ahead was to work out the proportion Pugin was using for the chancel. The dimensions were easy, 48 feet deep and 36 feet wide. Whilst I could see a mathematical connection, multiples of 12, there was no obvious proportion in use. A 48 foot deep chancel on top of a 120 foot nave didn't really give anything, apart from the nave being 2.5 times the size of the chancel.

One day, I took a walk along the centre line of the church, and stopped on the chancel at the point where the top line from the apse crosses the centre line. I was looking around to try and second-guess Pugin's intentions, when I happened to look down. I was absolutely amazed to find the floor tiles at that point appear to have been laid wrong. The whole thing made the hairs stand up on the back of my neck. [12]

---

[12] A colour photograph showing the tiles appears on the back cover of this book. [Eds.]

I went looking for something, and indeed found something at that spot. If you look at the point at which the line from the apse crosses the centre line of the church, you can see the errors in the tiles.

The picture shows that the central line crosses vertically, which is the centre line of the church. The diagonal line moving up from right to left is the 'setting out' line from the apse. At the intersection of the two lines there appears to be an error in the pattern of the tiles.

When I found the error on the tiles, I had gone to that point to look for something, so you can imagine my absolute surprise to actually find anything. The fact that I was following a 'trail' and found something of interest led me to believe this was not an error. The very precise, rather than random, errors also suggest a deliberate act and the Pugins were widely acclaimed for their tiles. Even if Pugin had made an error, surely Bro. Patrick would have put it right. I can't believe that the man who had carved the high altar in eighteen months would allow such an error in front of it. The picture below shows Patrick's magnificent altar and I've indicated the position of the error, which is under the rug behind the altar table.

If you look at the close up of the tiles, you can see that the top left hand square has to rotate through 90 degrees anti-clockwise and the right hand square 90 degrees clockwise. The left hand lower yellow triangle has to perform a flip/mirror image manoeuvre, with the right hand lower brown triangle. Effectively, the movements are taking place around the dots indicated.

If you drew a line between the top two dots, we have a line that is three small tiles in length and appearing to 'frame' the black cross below. Draw a line between the lower dots and you have a line five tiles wide. Both lines are then separated by four tiles.

3 4 5 is the classic Pythagorean triangle and so we have the proportion of the nave defined by the square root of five and that of the chancel by 5. Five and the square root of five occur frequently in 'sacred geometry' and holy sites around the world.

So was it an error or a message? For the reasons outlined above, I could not accept an error, so I photographed it and spent weeks thinking about it, again with endless scribbles, and finally decoded it. A flash of inspiration helped that night but I see now there was a more obvious answer that had been staring me in the face. If I had reduced the dimensions of the chancel from 36 feet by 48 feet to 3 by 4, then a 3,4,5, triangle would have been more obvious. Why did I get the inspiration that Friday night? Well, I don't know but, on the following Monday morning, the contractors were due to put a test pit into the chancel floor to find why the floor was sagging in various points. Perhaps somebody couldn't wait for me to find out the answer on my own, and sent the inspiration.

I also know that Pugin was using multiples of twelve, and if we assume that each two inch tile is equal to twelve feet, then the lines indicated start to give the dimensions of the chancel. 3 x 12ft = 36ft, which is the width of the chancel, 4 x 12ft = 48ft which is its depth, and 5 x 12ft = 60ft, which is the width of the nave.

Knowing the starting points, we can now construct a schematic diagram of the church and friary at a scale of 1:72.

It appears that someone had left behind a plan of the church proportions encoded in the pattern of tiles on the chancel floor. To this day, I am still astonished by this discovery and, at the time, it made me wonder who had done this? Was it Edward Pugin or Bro. Patrick? Much more likely to be Edward leaving his signature, but even so Bro. Patrick would have to know about it in order to correctly 'mislay' the tiles.

Painting of E.W.Pugin in All Saints Church, Barton-on-Irwell.

Working on the assumption that Edward was more likely to be the designer of the code, I visited All Saint's Church at Barton upon Irwell, designed by Edward Pugin, to see if he had done anything similar there. There was no evidence of anything on the chancel but there was on the nave walls. The nave is decorated with wall paintings, one of which depicts Lord and Lady de Trafford who founded the church, designed by Edward. In the entourage of people surrounding the de Traffords, Edward depicts himself. Edward records himself for posterity but just to make sure you know who he is, he carries a plan of the church so that everyone will know he is the architect.

I have been told that, at Scarisbrick Hall in Lancashire, which is designed by Edward's father, Edward had carried out alterations for Lady Scarisbrick including the addition of a library. In the stained glass of the library, Edward depicts Lady Scarisbrick with him, showing her a plan of the library. It would appear that Edward is leaving plans as his signature but at Gorton it is done in a much more subtle and imaginative way.

The question remains of Bro. Patrick's involvement. He must have known about the plan, perhaps a shared joke with Edward? So, I decided to find out more about this remarkable friar, who had built Gorton Monastery, extended the boys' school, built the girls' school, built the infant school and, in 1898, began building the two-storey St. Francis Parish Hall. In 1884, Bro. Patrick erected a workshop in the garden and, in the next eighteen months, had created the magnificent high altar designed by Peter Paul Pugin, Edward's stepbrother.

Chapter 10: In Search of Brother Patrick

Carving a name for 'himself'

Whilst I knew a lot of what Bro. Patrick had achieved, I knew little of the man himself. I located two articles written 100 years apart, which give some inkling of what Bro. Patrick was like.

*(*Extract from 'Among The Monks At Gorton', *The Free Lance,* April 6 1867*)*

"That" said our guide, pointing to one of the labourers who was pushing a stone into its place, "is one of the monks". "Is it possible?" "Oh yes" replied our host, "and he has saved us more than a thousand pounds. He is a good brick setter, a capital stone cutter, and he takes the place of a Clerk of the Works. You see, he cannot work in his habit so he puts on a workman's clothes." And there he was working like the rest of them, with his moleskin trousers, white blouse, and a flat cap over his tonsure. We thought of asking but didn't, whether he was a member of the trade's union. "But this is unusual, is it not?" we observed. "Oh no, not in history. It was thus that all our great abbeys were built, and we have found it a great advantage to revive the custom on a small scale."

A living link with the early days at Gorton was Miss Ellen Jackson who, at the age of 87, gave an interview to the Manchester Evening News in 1973. Miss Jackson was a pupil at St. Francis Infant School in 1892 and was appointed headmistress in 1923, retiring in 1950. The following text is her account of Bro. Patrick.

"She remembered many of the great figures of the past including one of the pioneer friars, Brother Patrick Dalton, who, with Father Willibrord was the hero of 26th September 1872, when the great Church of St. Francis was opened.

Speaking at the lunch that day, the architect Edward Welby Pugin described Brother Patrick not as Clerk of Works but as 'joint architect'. A tribute from a man who was not the easiest to work with.

Brother Patrick was even more than that. In the fifty years he served his Order, he was stone mason, wood carver, brick layer, cement maker and hod carrier. He did his stint of begging too, and was a well known figure in the local pubs with his collection box and his cry of "Let's buy another brick for St. Francis." He had his own way of recruiting volunteer labour: he met the men as they left work at midday on Saturday and asked for their help in the afternoon.

He supervised the building of the girls' school in 1877 and, between 1886 and 1893, was responsible for alterations and additions to the friary and other buildings. His masterpiece was the magnificent High Altar, designed by Peter Paul Pugin, which he began in 1894 and completed the following July.

The Parish Hall was his last task as Clerk of Works at Gorton in 1898 and he died in 1909, still in 'harness'.

Whilst giving me a fascinating glimpse of the man, it also gave the year of death. Using the internet, I searched for any Patrick Dalton death in 1909 and found only one. A Patrick Dalton death, at the age of 71, had been recorded in West Ham in the second quarter of 1909. The Franciscan friary at Forest Gate is located in West Ham, so presumably Bro. Patrick had died there, perhaps in retirement. I decided to look into Bro. Patrick's family history to see if this could shed any light on his background, and so looked up the census record for Gorton

Monastery for 1871. Brother Patrick, aged 34, was listed as Clerk of Works but disappointingly only gave 'Ireland' as his place of birth. Age 34 would have made his year of birth c1837 and was consistent with the death registration in West Ham.

A search of the internet records of Irish births revealed four possible records, two in Limerick and two in Wexford but none in Kerry, which Fr. Agnellus had identified as Bro. Patrick's birthplace. Never mind I thought, in following years the census requested where exactly you were born so I checked the 1881 Census. To my surprise, Brother Patrick was neither in Gorton nor elsewhere for that matter! So I checked the 1891 Census and he wasn't here, and then the 1901 Census and he still wasn't here! Very strange, he was here working for forty years by the evidence of the building works he was doing but whenever the census came around he had disappeared!

Puzzled by his absence from the census records, I began searching again for Irish records of Patrick Dalton from Kerry with no success. Around this time my friends Kath and Graham North, who have been invaluable volunteers with the Monastery over the years, came across a memorial at Moston Cemetery to the Franciscan Community Gorton. They had been researching Kath's family history when they found the memorial that contained the names of sixteen friars. Surprisingly, when they requested the details of the plot only the last four were listed as being buried there in the 1960s. I knew that there was a clergy vault in the cemetery used by the Salford of Diocese, so presumed the earlier burials had been in there or elsewhere. I searched for their deaths on the internet and found none of them, which was very strange. I then searched again but using last names only and found them all. Their deaths had been recorded under their legal Christian names. In life they had been known by their 'religious' names, chosen by them when they were professed into the Order. Problem solved, or was it?

The Community's grave in Moston Cemetery

It might have explained the Moston mystery but it raised further questions about Bro. Patrick. No amount of searching for Brother 'Patrick' Dalton's birth in Ireland would do any good if Patrick wasn't his Christian name but his religious name. Without his real name, I was at a loss as to what to do next.

Where there is despair, hope.

I looked again at all references to Bro. Patrick in Frs.
Agnellus' and Justin's books and noticed something odd. In
this extract from *Assisi to Gorton* 1938 by Fr. Agnellus
Andrew OFM, he gives an account of the attempt to speed up
progress on the church.[13]

*'Soon it was not enough for the men of the parish to come
and build their church. It was now necessary for them to come
and mount guard by night lest others might come and pull
down what they had so laboriously built up. No actual clash
ever took place between the Murphyites and our people but
night after night for months the men mounted guard on their
precious trust, Brother Patrick and the fathers with them most
of the time cheering them up, and at times quieting their excitement and resentment. Those days passed slowly and the work
went slowly on. Then in 1871 there was a sudden quickening of
the pace, with the election of Fr. Willibrord as Guardian. Let
me tell the story as I find it in the Archives of the Friary: 'On
the 14th of April, 1871, Frs. Gummair[14] and Willibrord began a
Mission at Batley in Yorkshire. Towards the end of the Mission
the Provincial Chapter was held in Belgium, and on the 1st of
May a telegram was received from Fr. Cuthbert containing the
following intelligence, 'Fr. Willibrord has been elected Guardian of Gorton, with Fr. Cuthbert as Vicar.' After a few
moments of agitation caused by the unexpected contents of this
telegram, Fr. Gummair and his new Superior packed up their
traps, bid good-bye to the parish priest of Batley, F. Bruno
Rigby, and set off for Gorton where they arrived 1st May 1871,
towards evening.'*

---

[13] Fr. Agnellus Andrew (1938)
[14] Actually this was Fr. Gommair. [Eds.]

Now notice how quickly things begin to move.

May 22nd - 'To-day, I (Fr. Willibrord) called on Michael Dalton to start work on the church. The work had been stopped for the past six months. The building was up to the height of the roof with the exception of the front and the chancel windows.'

May 26th - 'Not knowing how and where to find means for the completing of the church, I applied to Dr. Turner, Bishop of Salford.'

Why did Fr. Willibrord call Patrick 'Michael'? My mum, when calling my name out often, has to search through my brothers' names before she gets to mine – "Shaun, Brendan, Tony or whichever one you are...", but rarely in my experience do people write names down wrong. Could it be that Michael was Bro. Patrick's Christian name before joining the Order?

Could Willibrord have known Michael before he took his vows and his name in religion, Patrick? If so, had Willibrord been in Ireland?

I began to look for any evidence of Fr. Willibrord having been in Ireland. It turned out that Fr. Willibrord's surname was an absolute gift; there can't be many 'Willibrord van den Neuckers' wandering around Ireland in the 1860s. I was right. It didn't take long to find Fr. Willibrord arriving in Gorey, Co. Wexford in October 1858.

Under English rule, the Irish Franciscans had suffered a similar fate to their English brethren. By the end of the 18th century, the Irish Franciscan Province was at a low ebb and, in Rome, the Minister General was concerned that the Franciscans were not keeping to the regular observance of the rules of the Order. Again, the Belgian Province was asked to get involved and to found a Franciscan community, which would be a model for the Irish to follow.

In 1858, Mr Ram, a convert to Catholicism, offered land for the establishment of a religious Order in Gorey. As with Sclerder, Fr. Archangel Vendrickx, the Belgian Provincial, sent friars to help. Fr. Willibrord, accompanied by Fr. Victor Douterluigne and Bro. Lambert Heltzen. They took up residence in a house, on the Ramsfort estate, which they named St. Mary of the Angels. Fr. Victor was appointed Superior and was joined a year later by Fr. Patrick Verherstraeten, a young priest just four years ordained.

The Bishop of Ferns, Dr. Furlong, had been given temporary faculties in the diocese, but it soon became clear that no permission would be granted to open a public church in Gorey. There was resistance to the Franciscans from the local clergy who were not too impressed at having friars on their territory. Friars support themselves by begging, and hence the local clergy feared their own income would be diverted. Led by Fr. Patrick Verherstraeten, the friars left Gorey and arrived in Killarney in July 1860.

Fr. Victor and Bro. Lambert accompanied Fr. Patrick and they were joined by Fr. Eustace Princen. Tantalisingly, I now have the Belgian friars in Killarney, which is in Co. Kerry, the supposed county of Bro. Patrick's birth, but with no reference of Fr. Willibrord having been with them.

What was interesting was that Edward Pugin had also been in Killarney in 1855 to attend the opening of Killarney Cathedral. Had Bro. Patrick worked on the cathedral and come to the attention of Edward because of his fine workmanship? An intriguing possibility.

The Franciscans laid the first stone of the church, designed by Edward Pugin on the Feast of St. Patrick, 1864. Sadly, Fr.

Patrick died on Easter Sunday, 16th April 1865, before its completion. On the feast of the Portiuncula, 2nd August at 11 a.m., Solemn High Mass was celebrated in the newly completed church.

At this point, I was astounded to find the following description of the completion of the building works:

'The erection of the tower brought the construction of the Friary to a conclusion. This was designed by Pugin and Ashlin of Dublin. It stands at a height of 43 metres.

In 1878, Brother Patrick Dalton, a native of Glin, County Limerick, together with one mason and five labourers, set about constructing the tower. The stone for the main part of the building came from Killorglin and Firies, while the smooth stone of the belfry and spire came from Kanturk, County Cork. The upper stone-work was executed by Daniel McNamara, a skilled craftsman from Kanturk.

Outside the main door of the church, stands another work from the untiring hands of Brother Patrick: the stone holy water font still used by the faithful of Killarney.'

Killarney Friary

I had now found that Bro. Patrick not only worked tirelessly at Gorton for nearly forty years but also managed to take time off to go back to his native Ireland and complete another E.W. Pugin church and friary. Also the reference to being 'a native of Glin' finally solves the problem of Bro. Patrick's birthplace, Glin being a small village in County Limerick.

I began a new search for Michael Dalton, if my assumption about Fr. Willibrord's use of this name was right, and found only one entry for 1837, and this was recorded at Limerick where Glin is situated. The records office had been closed for lack of funding so, for now, the trail to Bro. Patrick was cold, so I decided to research other members of the Gorton community of friars. Before continuing that story, I would like to share what I thought at the time was a bizarre coincidence but now I am not so sure. As soon as I discovered Bro. Patrick's birthplace, I knew exactly where in Ireland it was.

In 2005 I went on a family holiday to Ireland, and spent Easter week at Kilkee on the west coast of Co. Clare. Whilst there, Gorton Monastery was often in my thoughts and I had this strange feeling that I would find something. It's hard to describe exactly.

One day we decided to take a day trip to Killarney, totally unconnected with my search for Bro. Patrick, which didn't begin in earnest till the end of 2005. This involved crossing the River Shannon by ferry to Tarbert in Kerry. I remember thinking of Bro. Patrick during the first part of that drive, perhaps because my subconscious was thinking what I believed was true at the time, which was that he was from Kerry or Killarney. My journey planner was to take the road from the ferry port to Tarbert, turn left for Glin 4 miles away, then turn right for Killarney. How strange that I should have been thinking of him in his birthplace.

Chapter 11: Fr. Cuthbert Wood

Mystery of the Carved Heads

In 'Assisi to Gorton', Fr. Agnellus tells us that, on the evening of the 25th September 1872, the day before the opening of the church, *'Father Cuthbert Wood, O.F.M, had blessed the new Church and now all was ready for the inaugural celebrations. All expectations were exceeded'*.

In 'Gorton Monastery 1861 – 1961', Fr. Justin McLoughlin tells us that, *'The Statues and Emblems in the Church were designed by Fr. Cuthbert Wood, O.F.M., and were executed by Messrs Williams and Wilson of Manchester.[15]'* Not only had Fr. Cuthbert designed the statues and emblems, he had also designed the magnificent crucifix hanging from the chancel arch.

The trail of Bro. Patrick had gone cold, so I decided to research Fr. Cuthbert. I found a reference by Fr. Justin that Fr. Cuthbert Wood, aged 58 years, had been appointed as a Definitor (Advisor) to the Provincial in 1891 and had been a Methodist convert from Hyde, Cheshire. The reference also noted that the initials O.F.M. (Order of Friars Minor) had replaced the earlier initials O.S.F. (Order of St. Francis). I did another search using his name and O.S.F., and it produced a surprising result. The link took me to the history of St. Cuthbert's Church, Maybole in Ayrshire, which had been opened in 1878.

From the web page I learnt that, on the exterior of the church, to the sides of the window arches, *'there are a series of sculptured representations of the late and present Popes;*

---

[15] Subsequent research has revealed that the company was actually called William Wilson & Co. [Eds.]

Cardinals Cullen, Manning, and Newman; the present Archbishops and Bishops of Scotland; Bishops Hay, Cameron, Scott, Gillis, Murdoch, Gray, and Lynch; Prior Vaughan, O.S.B., **Fr. Cuthbert Wood, O.S.F.,** *and Rev. M. Condon; Rev. Messrs. O'Shaughnessy, Thomson (deceased), and Dixon, pastors of Maybole; and Capt. Hunter Blair, Captain Kennedy, the Countess of Newburgh, and Madame l'Amirale Reynaud, of Brest.'[16]*

How strange! How and why did Fr. Cuthbert, in his own lifetime, come to have a sculpting of his head put on a church in Scotland alongside such illustrious companions including two Popes? The web page explained that *'local tradition has it that these heads were carved by an old tramp mason who turned up one day during the building of the church and asked for employment in hewing the stones. He proved to be so expert he was given the job of carving the heads to the arches and it is believed he modeled his carvings on the heads of some of his fellow workmen and carved one in his own image.'* [17]

---

[16] Extract from the Scottish Catholic Directory for 1880, quoted on the website of Maybole Community Council (updated 2011) *Welcome to Maybole, Ayrshire Scotland.* Available at:
http://www.maybole.org/community/churches/StCuthberts/history.htm
(Accessed 1st December, 2011.) [Eds.]

[17] Quoted on the above website, and taken originally from the book by James T. Gray (1972) *Maybole, Carrick's Capital*, Bale: Dragon Books. Chapter 12, page 123. [Eds.]

The carved head at Maybole Church.

Very odd that a man with such skill should have been a tramp[18] and I was doubly curious because we have six carved heads of friars below the arches leading into the nave from the porch at the Monastery. I've long suspected that Bro. Patrick had carved these as likenesses of his Franciscan brothers at Gorton. I also know Bro. Patrick, that remarkable 'beggar and builder', was known for scouring the streets of Manchester for unused bricks and begged in the local pubs for pennies to buy a brick for St. Francis. I wonder if that old tramp mason had been Bro. Patrick and the story had been corrupted over time.

---

[18] In fact the expression 'tramp mason' does not mean that the person was a tramp, but that he was self-employed, and 'tramped' from one building project to another. [Eds.]

Fr. Cuthbert Wood

So I continued my search for Fr. Cuthbert and I eventually came across a request on the internet for information concerning Fr. Cuthbert from a great-great-niece of his in Canada, Judy Buller. I contacted Judy and she had found Fr. Cuthbert Wood had managed to be recorded in two separate places in two consecutive census returns and was curious to know whether there were two Fr. Cuthbert Woods. And, if not, why was he being recorded in two places at the same time? Ironically, I had too few census returns for Bro. Patrick and Judy had too many for Fr. Cuthbert.

Judy provided a lot of information about Fr. Cuthbert, including dates of various ecclesiastical appointments and, for my part, I could provide a photograph of him. Fr. Cuthbert had been known as William Wood before he joined the Franciscans.

William Wood was born in 1833 in Hyde, Cheshire, England. By 1841, the family had moved to Fairfield Top Lock at Droylsden where his father was an engineer, presumably with the Ashton Canal.

In 1851, aged 17, William had moved to Openshaw, Manchester, where he was living with his widowed mother and some siblings. At this time he lists his occupation as 'draughtsman'. By 1861, William was still living with his widowed mother and a niece in Droylsden and records his occupation as 'medieval artist'.

Fr. Agnellus tells us that *'From the very first days of their coming to Gorton, the Franciscan Fathers devoted themselves with great zeal to the giving of Missions and Retreats. The first mission was given in Hyde in December 1862 by Frs. Willibrord and Germain, before they had been in England for a year. By 1865 they had made over 450 conversions to the faith through this work'*.

It is likely that, through this route, William Wood took the step to convert from Methodist to Catholicism and Franciscan. I can imagine how someone living in the simplicity and austerity of a Methodist household, but with an interest in medieval art, would be attracted by the sight of the Franciscans on the streets of Hyde. They would have appeared to him as 'romantic' medieval figures in the spirit of St. Francis. He joined them and was ordained as a priest in 1868, and took his name in religion – Cuthbert, and became part of the community at Gorton.

Once at Gorton, it would appear that Fr. Cuthbert used his obviously considerable skills as a draughtsman and medieval artist to design the statues and emblems in the church. His medieval influence is further evidenced by reference to his inspiration for the crucifix he designed, based on the Spanish Corpora Christi mentioned later.

Judy also told me that Fr. Cuthbert had been appointed Vicar to the community at St. Francis in Glasgow in 1874. Fr. Cuthbert was elected Guardian at St Francis, Glasgow in 1880 and 1883 and remained as Vicar there until 1894 at the latest. So I now knew that Fr. Cuthbert had been about forty miles from Maybole when the church was being built. I decided to check the census return for 1881 to confirm Fr. Cuthbert's presence and, sure enough, he was listed as R.C. Priest, 'head of household'. To my utter amazement, with him was Brother Patrick Dalton 'Clerk of Works.'

Not only had Bro. Patrick been Clerk of Works in Gorton, he had completed Killarney Friary and was now up in Scotland building another Franciscan friary.

In 1867, from Rutherglen to Govan (on the south side of the Clyde) the only Catholic church that was available for 20,000 Catholics was St John's, Portugal Street. Bishop John Gray, Vicar-Apostolic of the Western District of Scotland, resolved to ease the position by asking Papal permission to establish a new parish, which was granted. The Bishop, on 29th September 1868, formally invited Fr. Emmanuel Kenners from Gorton to establish a friary in Glasgow. The boundaries of the proposed Franciscan parish were agreed on 16th November, and the friar's first home was at Wellington Place, at the corner of Commercial Road.

The first Community consisted of Frs. Emmanuel, Martin Verhagen (brother of Fr. Francis, the first Guardian at Gorton), Bertrand and Brendan Butti; you may recall that Thomas Butti and Stephen Prendergast had been students with the Franciscans at Sclerder. Now named Brendan and Jarlath respectively, they, with Cuthbert Wood and Aidan Morris, were the first British subjects ordained for the Franciscans after their return to the British Isles. Their ordination took place at Liege, on 6th June 1868. Also joining their brothers in Glasgow, Frs. Innocent Bulens, Bertrand Schultze, Anselm Knapen, and Antonine Scannell; all of them 'alumni' of Gorton Monastery.

In November, Bro. Patrick was sent for from Gorton, and a small chapel built by him was opened and dedicated to St. Francis on the Third Sunday of Advent (13th December 1868). In just four weeks Bro. Patrick, with the help of the Catholics, had completed the little chapel and, within the next two weeks, the first baptism and marriage took place.

The Glasgow Friary

The erection of the friary was begun on 14th February 1869, and opened as a temporary chapel on 11th July, of the same year, the former building having proved too small. The original chapel was converted to a school.

The previous picture shows the friars outside the newly opened chapel in Glasgow and, unless I'm very much mistaken, I would say that Bro. Patrick is the figure on the left and I would hazard a guess that Fr. Cuthbert is the portly figure third from the left.

In April 1874, to the keen regret of all, Fr. Emmanuel resigned his office due to ill health and returned to Belgium. He was a friar of outstanding dignity and merit, and was held in great respect by all. For sixteen years he had led his 'pioneers' from Sclerder to Killarney, Gorton and Glasgow.

Father Emmanuel Kenners, O.F.M.

Fr. Gommair followed him as Guardian and held office until 8th December 1878, when on a visit to his native place (Lierre), he died. Fr. Cuthbert succeeded him and continued in office until April 1884. Before continuing the story of Fr. Cuthbert and Bro. Patrick in Scotland, I'd like to share the story of Fr. Gommair.

Fr. Gommair and Alice Ingham

Whilst at Gorton, Fr. Gommair had met Alice Ingham, a Rochdale woman, who had been professed into the Third Order at Gorton Monastery, wished to establish a religious community, and was frustrated by the period of probation required of them. She confessed this one day at the Monastery and the priest, hearing her confession, offered to be her spiritual director. She thanked him, finished her confession and left. On leaving, she realised she had no idea who her confessor was and returned to read his name on the confessional door; Fr. Gommair Peeters. Fr. Gommair was true to his word and continued to support Alice even after he left for Glasgow, and she had gone to London at the invitation of Bishop Vaughan in 1878, writing regularly to her with encouragement and support.

Fr. Gommair Peeters

Alice Ingham

In his last letter, he had told her he would try to visit her in London on his way to the Provincial Chapter in Belgium.

Sadly, he did not manage to visit and died before his return; the community in Glasgow were advised as follows.

'Very Reverend Father Gommair Peeters, Guardian of Glasgow, who took part in the already mentioned Chapter, and there was re-elected for a third time as Guardian to the same friary at Glasgow, before his departure from Belgium, became afflicted by a lethal disease and died a pious death on 8th December 1878 at Lierre, the town of his birth. May he rest in Peace.'

Fr. Polycarp Vervoort at Gorton continued Fr. Gommair's role as spiritual director for Alice and on the 8th September 1883, Alice, now Mother Francis, and eleven of her companions all of whom were professed members of the Franciscan Third Order, made Religious Vows of Poverty, Chastity and Obedience. They became Sisters of St. Joseph's Society. Their Franciscan Spirit was fostered by the friars at Stratford, London. The Stratford 1882 Trade Directory lists Rev. Francis Verhagen, Rev. Germain Verleyen, Rev. Aidan McCarthey (Guardian), Rev. W. James Egan, Rev. Bede Wrigley and Rev. Columban Ellison as being present at the Catholic Church of St. Francis of Assisi, Grove Crescent Road, Stratford. Mother Francis would, therefore, have been amongst good friends as all had been at Gorton in the 1860s and 70s. In Gorton, Fr. Francis was the first Guardian, Fr. Germain celebrated their first Christmas Mass and Fr. Aidan who, as William McCarthy, had been an altar boy and student at Gorton, became the first Manchester born boy to become a Franciscan priest at Gorton.

The story of Fr. Gommair and Alice reminds me of St. Francis and his spiritual direction of St. Clare all those years ago in Assisi.

Fr. Polycarp

Fr. Polycarp was the Professor of Theology at the Seraphic College in the friary at Gorton. The entire Seraphic College was transferred from Gorton to St Bernardine's College, Buckingham, on 11th October 1895. Whether the transfer of his beloved boys had anything to do with it or not, for he had been a most fatherly and successful Rector of the little College, Fr. Polycarp Vervoort was found dead in his room at Gorton on the 29th November 1896. He left behind him the well earned reputation of being a very great priest, ordained in 1849, Commissary of the Holy Land in Great Britain for many years, and truly one of the Franciscan pioneers who built up the church and parish in Gorton, and the Order in England. He was Provincial 1893 to 1896, and the author of a manuscript History of the Restoration of the Order in England. He is buried in the Clergy vault at Moston cemetery, Manchester. His name is, however, also recorded on the memorial to the Franciscan Community there.

Back to Glasgow and on to Chilworth, Surrey.

Fr. Alexander Murphy tells us that *'In November 1877, through the Glasgow City Bank failure, £1,500, which had been lodged towards the building of a new church, was lost. The work, however, proceeded with, and Brother Patrick was brought from Killarney as master of works. It was at this time the writer had the pleasure of seeing him at work, and he had set down his impressions on page 63 of 'A Spiritual Retreat'. On February 2nd 1880, the first sod was cut; on 25th May the foundation stone was laid by His Grace, Archbishop Eyre, and in October the vast building was roofed in. On 31st May 1881, His Eminence Cardinal Manning preached for the opening.'*[19]

---

[19] The original source of this passage is unknown. The book referred to was published in 1920 as *A Spiritual Retreat* by Fr. Alexander, O.F.M. Burns, Oates & Co.: London. [Eds.]

I can imagine how sad Fr. Cuthbert would have been to lose his Brother from their Gorton days, and how diligent he was in picking up the reins.

Chilworth Friary

The Foundations of the present church building were laid in 1880. This replacement building, by the architects Pugin & Pugin, in Early Decorated style, was magnificent, visually and acoustically.

On the 2nd February 1880, the first sod of earth was turned on the same site as the smaller original church with the foundation stone being laid at a ceremony on the 25th May 1880. The original drawings submitted were altered due to a lack of funding, with the proposed massive tower and side transepts taken out. The formal opening took place on the 1st June 1881, the building having taken only 16 months to construct.

Judy had also told me that Fr. Cuthbert had been Guardian at Chilworth Friary, so I began to search the internet for more details about Chilworth.

According to one website, in 1887, Fr. David Fleming, the new Provincial, began to look for a new site to build a novitiate house. In 1889, a site was found at Blackheath on a lane leading up from Chilworth in Surrey. In May the following year, Fr. Bonaventure Brierton and Fr. William Price moved into a cottage nearby in preparation of building the friary. And then, to my complete astonishment, the story continued and revealed that in *'October 1890 Bro. Patrick Dalton, a Limerick man who had been involved in the building and furnishing of Glasgow Manchester and Forest Gate friaries became the clerk of works. A great tribute to the fine workmanship of this devoted man is the fact that 100 years later the friars are still using the refectory tables he constructed.'*[20]

Not only could I add Chilworth to the list of friaries constructed by Bro. Patrick, I could now add Forest Gate as well. The story of Chilworth Friary continued, and I learnt that Fr. Bede Wrigley and Bro. Patrick were able to move into the east wing of the friary on the 21st November 1891, and that the church was consecrated and opened in June 1892.

My curiosity about the carved stone heads in Maybole had led me to learn that Bro. Patrick, as well as his astounding feats of building in Gorton and his tireless work in Killarney, had been responsible for building one other chapel and three more

---

[20] This extract was taken from the 'St. Francis Gorton Honour Roll' website (updated 2007). Available at:
http://www.freewebs.com/liverpoolannie/apps/photos/photo?photoid=26289 520 (Accessed 1st December, 2011). The original source of the material is not acknowledged. [Eds.]

Franciscan churches and friaries. The mystery of the carved heads remains but certainly both of them had been in Scotland together at the time the Maybole church was being built.

Judy had been unable to find Fr. Cuthbert's death certificate and final resting place but did have the date. Remembering my experience with the Franciscans at Moston, I searched for William Wood aged 80 at death and got just two results, one of which was recorded at Hambledon close to Chilworth Friary. Through a contact associated with Chilworth Friary, Aileen Lawrence, I asked her to see if Fr. Cuthbert was buried in burial ground at the friary. Within days, Aileen had located and photographed his grave, although his year of birth was wrong.

Chapter 12: Fr. Francis Verhagen

The Wreck of the Deutschland

As well as the churches and friaries worked on by Bro. Patrick, I knew that the Franciscans had established themselves in Stratford, London. At the opening ceremony, at Gorton in 1872, Archbishop Manning expressed his wish to have a Franciscan presence in London. He offered the Franciscans possession of a recently completed church, St. Vincent de Paul in Grove Crescent Road, Stratford, for which Edward Pugin had been the Clerk of Works. Fr. Francis Verhagen, the first Guardian at Gorton, was appointed the Parish Priest and, with Bro. Patrick, took up residence there in 1873, the church then being re-dedicated to St Francis.

The wreck of the SS Deutschland was the subject of a famous poem by Gerard Manley Hopkins, who was born nearby in Stratford.

The SS Deutschland had sailed from Bremerhaven on the 4th December 1875, bound for New York via Southampton. The following day, in appalling weather, she ran aground on a sandbank about 25 miles from Harwich. For nearly thirty hours the ship lay stranded, taking on water and being pounded mercilessly by the waves. On the morning of the 6th, the order was given to abandon ship and distress rockets were fired, only to be ignored by passing ships. Only two lifeboats were launched, one of which foundered straight away, whilst the other drifted ashore the following day with just one survivor. At last the alarm was raised and it took another thirty hours before a tug reached them and rescued 135 survivors; another 78 had died from drowning or, in most cases, from hypothermia.

Amongst those who died were five Franciscan nuns escaping from anti-Catholic laws in Westphalia, Germany to begin a new life in the Americas. In an article in *The Times* from the 11th of December, the nuns are described: *'Five German nuns, whose bodies are now in the dead-house here, clasped hands and were drowned together, the chief sister, a gaunt woman 6 ft. high, calling out loudly and often 'O Christ, come quickly!' till the end came.'*

The 'dead-house' referred to was the school hall underneath the Church of St. Francis in Stratford. Fr. Francis, together with another priest, had recovered the bodies of five of the nuns from Harwich, one other being missing at sea, and brought them to Stratford. The death of the Franciscan nuns caused national outrage amongst the Catholics because no one had come to their aid in time. Cardinal Manning agreed to be present and speak at the funeral presided over by Fr. Francis and fifty other priests. The nuns, washed and freshly dressed, lay 'in state' at Stratford until the day of the funeral. Fr. Edwin Whitsker wrote an account of the funeral for the *Franciscan Monthly* and estimated the crowds lining the streets from Stratford to St. Patrick's Cemetery at Leytonstone to be forty thousand!

In 2007, I went to St. Patrick's Cemetery and found the memorial to the nuns and its inscription:

Pray for the Souls of Barbara Hultenschmidt, Henrica Fassbender (not found), Norberta Reinkober, Aurea Badziura, and Brigitta Damhorst, Franciscan Nuns from Germany. Who were drowned near Harwich in the wreck of the Deutschland Dec 7th, 1875. Four of whom were interred here December 13th. R.I.P

The grave of the Franciscan Nuns, at Stratford.

My search for an obituary.

In 2006, I gave a tour and the organiser brought a carrier bag with him full of his Gorton memorabilia, which included an obituary card for Fr. Arthur, another 1960s Friar. After the tour, I couldn't get the word 'obituary' out of my head for hours and hours. So I stopped and thought about it for a while and then the lights came on; there must have been obituaries for Patrick, Francis, Willibrord and their brothers; blindingly obvious but something I'd missed out on during my search.

The following day I set off for the Manchester Central Library to look for copies of *The Harvest*, the Catholic newspaper of the time. I know that Bro. Patrick died in the quarter Apr-Jun 1909 but had never got around to getting his death certificate, as it wouldn't have the same relevance as it might to family historians, who then get leads to next of kin. But I have always been aware that this was remiss of me and that I should really find the exact date of his death at Forest Gate and his burial place. For some reason, however, all the way to the library, I couldn't get June 1909 out of my head and asked for that year book, and also 1911 to check something else. I fully expected to find Bro. Patrick's obituary.

Whilst waiting for the books to come up from the basement, I went to the Catholic shelves, saw a book on Cardinal Vaughan who had some involvement with Gorton, and picked it up to open it on a page discussing Fr. Gommair Peeters and his link to Alice Ingham. From this I learnt their story, and was able to get a picture of Alice Ingham.

The Harvest arrived and, with bated breath, I turned to June 1909 and there on the front page was the notice of Fr. Francis Verhagen's death; not Patrick's as I had expected. Where did he come from? Fr. Francis was the very first Guardian at Gorton, and the paper reported his death but due to timing wouldn't be able to publish his obituary till the following month. I turned to this and read details of his life from his origins in Holland to his dying hours. And a photo of the dear old grey haired man to go with the fresh faced 'crusader' I already have.

The Late, Very Reverend Fr. Francis, O.F.M.

'By the death of Father Francis there has passed away one whose genial smile and whose encouraging words will be missed by so many readers of The Harvest; for although his vocation chained him to his home in the Friary, Gorton, his confessional was the goal of many a pilgrim in search of peace, consolation, strength and enlightenment. For many years his life was, comparatively, a hidden one, but as it was a life hidden in God it became more and more fruitful as Father Francis advanced in age: his advices were mellowed with the wisdom of the Holy Spirit that had been filtering through years of prayer, meditation, close observation of men and manners, and all who had recourse to him felt that, when he spoke, they were imbibing something more than the wisdom of the mere man – they felt that they were rather favoured with oracular messages from above.

Such results, as a general rule, are the outcome only of a life wholly devoted to God. The average man may know the Science of the Saints, but it is only he who follows and is imbued with the Science that can allure others to the life of union with God. It is a life hard to flesh and blood. To be induced to follow it, one requires more than the mere pointing out of the way – the guide himself must have trod every inch. This was the case with Father Francis, and it accounts for his great influence with souls; they felt they were being guided by one who was perfectly familiar with the difficulties of the spiritual journey, and who had tasted some of the sweets given by God to those who love Him.

Fr. Francis Verhagen O.F.M. (1832 – 1909)

The subject of our too short memoir was born at Wert, Holland, on 14th February, 1832, and until he entered the Franciscan Order in Belgium was known as Paul Verhagen. He was clothed with the habit of St. Francis at Thielt, West Flanders, on 4th October, 1848, and after his profession there, *on 5th October 1849, he followed the usual course of studies at Reckheim, Ghent, and St. Trond, and was ordained priest at Liege on 2nd June 1855. He was very proud of having studied Moral Theology under Father Pius Van der Velden, O.F.M., a theologian of great merit, whose works Father Francis regretted were not better known.*

Father Francis was a fellow student of the late Father Emmanuel Kenner's, O.F.M., and with him and a few others came to England about the 'sixties'. From that time until his decease, he took a leading part in the history of the Friars Minor in England. Conspicuous for his prudence, his urbanity, his piety, and his business tact, he repeatedly held office of the Superior in Stratford (London), Glasgow, and Manchester, and always to the satisfaction of the Bishops of the diocese, his confreres, and the people. He was noted for his respect for the secular clergy, and for his deep reverence towards the Episcopate. In the metropolis, he won the lasting esteem of the late Cardinals Manning and Vaughan, and in the Provinces his devoted work merited the warm approval of His Grace the Archbishop of Glasgow and his Lordship the Bishop of Salford.

Of late years he held the onerous position of Commissary of the Holy Land, and his devotion to this great work literally knew no bounds; indeed, his last letters, written within a couple of hours of his death, were in the interest of the Holy Places, and last year he saw through the press the English edition of the 'Guide to the Holy Places', which was the last of a series of publications he had been instrumental in bringing under the notice of the public.

His last hours were in perfect harmony with the other actions of his long life - they were well ordered, serene, prayerful, and dutiful. Surrounded by his loving brethren he received the Visitcum, and was anointed at 10.45 a.m. on Friday 18th June 1909, (the Feast of the Most Sacred Heart of Jesus). At 4.30 *p.m. he laid down his pen for the last time. After dinner he had a friendly chat and a quiet game of dominoes with three of the elder brethren, and at 7.35 p.m., as gently as a child, he yielded up his spirit into the hands of the Creator, as his sorrowing brethren were reciting the prayers for the dying. May he rest in Peace'.*

Fr. Alexander, O.F.M.

The article then continued with details from the Education Committee meeting giving further accounts of Fr. Francis' life.

At a meeting of the Gorton Education Committee on Tuesday, June 29th, the Chairman (Alderman W. H. Wainwright, J.P.), referred to the death of the Reverend Fr. Francis Verhagen of the Friary, Gorton. He said that Fr. Francis was a man of noble character. He was once a colleague of theirs on that committee, and the first representative from St. Francis when the 1902 Education Act came into operation. To many of them, the Reverend Father was not intimately known and, although he was not a member of the same Church as Fr. Francis, he claimed to have known the Reverend Father longer than most of those who would call themselves old Gortonians. He remembered the Franciscans building the great and beautiful church in Gorton Lane amongst the tall poplars, and he knew the active work of Fr. Francis and Bro. Patrick for over 30 years. His early public life as a young man brought him in close touch and conversation with both. When he heard the Reverend Fr. Bede give out, as his text, 'That man was perfect and upright, and feared God and eschewed evil,' he was struck with the appropriateness of the text. Fr. Francis was always anxious, earnest, and devoted to the spiritual and intellectual welfare of the children committed to his care, and zealously sought to make their conditions of life as pure and as bright as possible; whilst with adults he was intensely earnest as to their spiritual and temporal welfare. He was always ready to help and guide wherever necessary, and by his tender care and watchfulness many had been helped. He was a broad, intelligent administrator, true friend, wise counsellor and agreeable colleague. Gortonians were all the richer for such a life having been spent amongst them and all the poorer now it had passed away. All they could do was to try to follow the example he had set them, and express and place on record their admiration and high appreciation for the noble and valuable services rendered to the district – spiritually, morally, and intellectually. He moved the following resolution:-

> *"That this committee desire to express their sincere sympathy and condolence with the Rev. Father Jerome and his colleagues at the Monastery, Gorton, on the death of the Rev. Father Francis, who served on this committee during its first year of office as the representative of the Roman Catholic schools in the district."*

Councillor Bushell, in seconding the resolution, referred to the noble work of the Reverend Fr. Francis during his many years' stay in Gorton.

The resolution was carried.

Fr. Jerome, in returning thanks, said that he and his colleagues of the friary appreciated the kind expressions that had been made about the late Fr. Francis. They were especially pleased at the kindness and respect always shown to Fr. Francis in his work in Gorton by members of the other denominations.[21]

But what did all this have to do with Patrick? I turned to 1911 to look up an article about the Jubilee celebrations at Gorton. I had a copy of this already but was prompted to look at the original. There was a line above the article that said

---

[21] From *The Harvest*, July 1909. [Eds]

'following on from last month's story', and then the story of which I have a copy. So I turned to the previous month and it was a sort of warm up to the event describing how the friars at Gorton would be celebrating their 50th anniversary. Contained in the article was this priceless gem: 'Fr. Francis with his greatest friend Bro. Patrick Dalton worked tirelessly in the building of Gorton Monastery...' etc. My search for Patrick had led me directly to the life and work of Fr. Francis, about whom I knew some of the things but very little about the man himself. Almost as if I was pointed in his direction as being important in my story, which in time proved to be so true.

The following day, I received a message from somebody at the Council whose colleague had been on my tour and was on holiday in Killarney, Ireland. She passed on her mobile number and asked if I wanted anything looking up while she was there. I had been working with another great-great-niece, Celia, on the life of a Lancashire Friar who died quite young and had been at Gorton in Cuthbert's time. We had put most of his story together, including his obituary (but again I hadn't picked up on the importance of this at the time). She hadn't been able to put him to rest without knowing where he was buried, which, we thought, would be at Killarney Friary as they have a cemetery like Chilworth, but neither of us had managed to check this. I sent Celia the details of Fr. Frederick Eccles and, on an impulse, asked her to look out for Frs. Willibrord van den Neucker and Bruno de Grave, both of whom seem to have disappeared off the face of the earth after the opening of the Monastery in 1872. Celia proved to be a star and produced photos of all three graves together with a contact e-mail of a Franciscan who might be able to help. Where had Willibrord been for the 30 years till his death? I have since discovered that his gift of oratory meant that he was more suited to preaching and conversion work than parochial life, and spent much of his time across the UK on this mission. He died suddenly whilst on holiday in Killarney.

I e-mailed the contact, not expecting a reply, and was pleasantly surprised to get a speedy response. Surprised for two reasons, firstly, I was speaking to the Provincial of the whole Irish Province and, secondly, he had spent some time at Gorton in 1969. Whoopee! He thanked me for the brief history and pictures I sent him as he loves history, but feared he couldn't help too much. One gem, though, was the fact that Killarney was under the jurisdiction of the Belgian province until the 1890s and there might be some information there. He also gave me the details of his archivist who might be able to help as 'he is a mine of information'.

On the 6th June I had an e-mail from the Irish archivist before I'd even had a chance to write to him, as he'd been copied into my earlier e-mail. He confirmed that Patrick had never been a member of the Irish Province and had been professed into the Belgian Province, and where there might be records. (By another coincidence I found the Belgian archivist a few weeks earlier and somebody here who speaks Flemish). Fr. Ignatious also confirmed that Bro. Patrick died at Forest Gate in 1909 and went on to give the date 11th June – which was the coming Monday. After all these years of looking for him, he turns up just before his feast day and weeks before we are due to complete the restoration. Fr. Ignatious then dropped the second bombshell - he believed that Patrick was buried at Chilworth. Can you hear them chuckling? I e-mailed Aileen, who found Cuthbert for me, and she promised to take a look over the weekend. I had been trying to get a look up at Leytonstone, the nearest cemetery to Forest Gate, but it looked like I was searching in the wrong direction.

But why no obituary for the famous Bro. Patrick in the Salford Diocese newspaper? Surely somebody would have thought to do it even though he died in London. The answer is quite simple. His greatest friend, Fr. Francis, who surely would have done it, was himself dying and passed away just a week later on 18th June.

Reverend Fr. Frederick Eccles

Before moving on, I would like to include the obituary of Fr. Frederick Eccles, whose grave I had suspected was in Killarney.

The Chorley Standard, Saturday 22nd January 1887.

There died last week, at the Friary Killarney, from typhus fever, contracted in the midst of pastoral duties, the Rev. Frederick Eccles, son of Mrs. Eccles, of Market Street Chorley. The deceased priest was well-known as an earnest and energetic worker, and his early death is deeply deplored by a large circle.

On Sunday last, Father Bonaventure preached a funeral sermon at the Friary Chapel, Killarney. He said: Father Frederick was born of an old Catholic family, viz., Eccles, of Chorley, in Lancashire, on the 12th November 1844, so that he was in the 43rd year of his age. He made his classical studies at the Salford Catholic Grammar School, from within the walls of which several eminent men have issued. He joined the Franciscan Order in 1867, and made his profession on 16th October. From 1868 until 1873, he was raised to the highest dignity of the priesthood, at Mechlin, the metropolitan City of Belgium.

He returned from the Convent immediately after his ordination, and his first mission was Stratford, in the East of London. Here he began a career which, from the beginning to the end, throughout the whole length and breadth of it, has been singularly marked by burning zeal, and blended with the deepest humility. You were all witnesses to his zeal. A fortnight ago he crawled into this pulpit, though the fever had already parched his throat, and was causing him the most terrific pains in the head. Was he not in that Confessional a few days ago? Oh! Really, he was struck down with the arms in his hand.

Fr. Frederick only remained a short time at Stratford, where his principle duty consisted in burying the dead. There is a very large cemetery attached to the Mission of Stratford, and sometimes in a single day the funerals number twenty or thirty. This was his work day after day, ardent as was his zeal; his humility was so great that he thought the Father could not have chosen a work more fitting for him. Someone had to do it; was he not the member of the community least apt for the mission, least qualified for parish duty? Consequently, the cemetery work always devolved upon him rightly so. Such were the

117

sentiments of our dear departed father and friend; many the times has he in his artless way expressed himself to that effect.

From Stratford he was sent to Manchester, where for more than eight years he laboured in the parish of West Gorton. The Catholics scattered over this wide district are almost without exception of the labouring class, most of them mill hands working in the factories. Here it was that the gentle unassuming young priest affected marvellous changes in the flock committed to his charge; night and day he was always ready at their call. Nor did he wait till sent for, but, like the Good Shepherd, he went in search of the lost sheep, and brought them back to the sacraments, sometimes having to use gentle force.

Among the non-Catholics, he was universally respectful. His zeal was so well known that it almost passed into a proverb. Let me give you an instance of it: there was a poor Protestant woman sick unto death of the small-pox; the minister was sent for, but on learning the nature of the disease he refused to go, saying it would be too great a risk for a man with a wife and family. The Protestant of the neighbourhood then sent for the little Catholic priest. Father Frederick rushed to the poor woman. What a risk! The neighbours had insisted upon the windows and doors of the sick room being closed, lest the contagion should spread. Here Fr. Frederick remained by the bedside of the woman in the last stage of small-pox. She was as black as coal from the disease. Here he remained for over an hour, telling her about the real religion. So struck was the poor creature by the priest's heroism, that she asked to be admitted to the Catholic Church; and hardly had Father Frederick finished his ministrations when she died, quite reconciled, and even happy. Father Frederick took the small-pox, and nearly lost his life; thus he was a martyr of charity; but he had done his duty, what did he care? One instance like this reveals the whole man.

Since he has been in Killarney, he has been winning golden opinions in town and country; at how many death-beds has he given comfort that none but a really zealous priest can impart? There is one more trait in Fr. Frederick's character which cannot be passed over; it was his fatherly love for little children. Whenever obedience placed him, the little children flocked around his confessional, went to him with their little troubles; in Manchester the care of the children's confraternity was confided to him; and with what loving solicitude did he watch over his charges? Not only did he minister to their spiritual wants, but to what lengths did he not go in order to promote a little enjoyment – some little entertainment – for the little ones? He would forget himself entirely for them, become one of themselves; and all he sought in return for the time and trouble expended, was to see the joy beaming in their little faces. Now, my dear brethren, is it not safe to say that the zeal of a priest who labours for the children is a disinterested zeal? When those children have become men and women, the priest who guarded their childhood's years will have passed away. Is it not, "Others have laboured, you enter on the fruits of their labour; others have sown the seed, you enjoy the fruits of the harvest?"

Finally - and this is the cause of all his success at home and abroad, doing parish duty or giving missions; oh, how he was loved by the people to whom he gave missions! Finally, I say, Fr. Frederick was a true son of our Holy Father, St. Francis; he was a Franciscan to his heart's core. Humility and simplicity characterised his work on earth, and when he was told to prepare for the last – and for him, let us hope, the best – home, his Franciscan spirit supported and strengthened him. Was he dismayed when he was told to prepare for the last sacraments? Never was the warning received with greater calm. With unruffled sweetness, he received the summons, those who attended him can vouch for that sweet calm preserving to the end. His death was the fit crowning of his life; a calm, peaceful life points to a calm, peaceful death. He has gone from amongst us; never more will you listen to his voice from this pulpit; never more will he speak those burning words in your ear from the confessional. But will he be forgotten, therefore? No; a thousand times the people cherish longer the memory of their departed fathers in God than in this town and neighbourhood. Father Frederick knew this, and many a time did he say that he sincerely hoped to die in Killarney. He has had his wish soon, much too soon for us. Do not belie his hopes; why did he wish to die in your midst? Because he knew of your affectionate remembrance of the departed. While in life he looked forward to this remembrance. Oh, give it him fully and unreservedly; he loved you as no one but a priest of God can love; he loved your souls, and for that was ready to risk his life and health. Show a return of love by your fervent prayers for his soul; show that your love is stronger than death.

Chapter 13: Calvary

The lead to Chilworth cemetery had been wrong. A simple phone call to the cemetery, however, revealed that Bro. Patrick was buried in the Franciscan plot at St Patrick's, Leytonstone, London on the 15th June 1909, the anniversary was to be the coming Friday.

So on the 11th June, I lit lots of candles on the now derelict altar that had been carved by Bro. Patrick in just 18 months, and spent some time on my own in the church, celebrating the life of a man I had grown to love yet never known.

Back at my desk that day, I decided I would send for his death certificate, although I knew it wouldn't give any information about his origins, just his cause and place of death. That is all I gleaned from Fr. Cuthbert's certificate. Before ordering the certificate online, I received a phone call asking for me by name from a priest in Cheshire. Some of his parishioners had taken part in one of my tours over the weekend and they were enthusing about it in his company. He was surprised as he knew Gorton Monastery was closed in 1990 and hadn't heard about the restoration. He knew of the closure because some years after he had purchased statues of Our Lady, Mary Magdalene and St. John to create a Calvary scene at his church in Telford. He had them restored and set up in his church. The vendor provided the providence of the objects, including their manufacture in Paris in 1900 and their installation at Gorton Monastery.

He had since left Telford and the church was now closed. He believed that the statues had now been transferred to an army barracks chaplaincy, and he would provide details of the parish priest. He thought they were planning a new church and that the statues would be too large.

He gave me the details of the parish priest at Telford and, as soon as I finished the call, I rang Telford.

I then rang the army chaplain, Fr. Bill, and told him my tale, and he confirmed he was their custodian and that they were getting in the way. All we had to do was send 'a man and a van' and they were ours.

Whoopee! Absolute elation! You cannot believe how overjoyed I was, no I am. Nice story I can hear you thinking, good bit of luck, but not exactly earth shattering. Well you are wrong there - it is the most stunning news I have come across in my five year search into Bro. Patrick and his colleagues.

On the anniversary of Patrick's death, not only do we locate the statues but we are promised them back at no cost. Life doesn't get any better than that! You would have thought by now that I should know better than that – at Gorton Monastery anything is possible. I went home elated at the day's events and, logging on later in the evening, I received another e-mail from Ireland asking if I was aware that there used to be a Calvary scene at Gorton Monastery. Just in case, he offered some information about its history:

'In May 1919, a Calvary, the gift of Sir Richard Holden, in memory of Brother Patrick Dalton, was erected near the porch.'

You could not have scripted a more fitting fairy tale ending to my search for Bro. Patrick. On the anniversary of his death, having celebrated his life we are given the location of the statues, promised them back free of charge, and only then do we discover that they were a memorial to him erected to celebrate the tenth anniversary of his death. Priceless!

My problem now is about who Patrick was. I've always been nervous about him being recorded as Patrick in the death registration at Leytonstone. All his colleagues were listed under their real names. I had mistakenly thought he was Michael turned Patrick, now it appears he was Patrick turned Michael. In the wealth of documentation from Ireland, I can see the error in the 1924 manuscript. Subsequent chroniclers have clearly used this source and therefore the error persisted. Writers who didn't know him personally used the only name they had, 'Patrick'. Only Fr. Willibrord referred to him as Michael. This was the red herring that led me to Ireland, and ultimately to all the subsequent discoveries. I believed Willibrord must have known him as Michael and, therefore, had to have been in Ireland long enough to get know him as that. Wrong. It now turns out that Patrick was professed into the Order on 12th November 1861 as a Tertiary (Third Order), a civilian for want of easy description - bound to the Franciscan rule but not required to live in the cloister unless he chose. Pictures you've seen of him show him wearing the scapula as an old man but also as a young man c1868. This can only be worn if he was professed into the First Order. Patrick must have been professed at Gorton 1862/68 and taken the name Michael, and Willibrord is therefore correct in using that.

One reason for professing Tertiaries was to harness their skills for the benefit of the Order. Within days of entering the Order, Patrick was on his way to Gorton arriving two weeks later. Clearly a man on a mission, but who sent him/called him, who knew he was the man for the job? I contacted the Belgian Franciscan archive and got a very nice prompt reply, 'very little English Province records survive in Belgium.'

Chapter 14: Franciscan Crown

Our Lady Queen of Peace

People often comment on how lucky or clever we have been in recovering treasures lost from the Monastery. In truth, the treasures have found us through coincidences and happenchance, each one more and more astounding than the last. A man came to see us who had been an altar boy in the 1970s at Gorton. He gave us a Rosary, which had been given to him by Bro. Gerard in 1971 and was then at least 50 years old. It has wooden beads about the size of a marble and is about 3 feet long.

The Franciscans wore a rosary at the waist. The Franciscan rosary is different from all the rest as it has seven decades rather than five.[22] Each decade requires saying ten Hail Marys and seven decades gives seventy Hail Marys. You follow it by two more to give 72 - the number of years Our Lady is supposed to have lived on Earth. It is known as the Franciscan Crown and dates back to 1422.

The number 72 was running through my head for a few days afterwards, and it occurred to me that Pugin's mysterious tiles on the chancel floor were at a scale of 1:72. Was Pugin alluding to this? I decided to check the reference to Our Lady's age being 72 and typed '72 years our lady' into a search engine. Up came the first ten websites but one in particular caught my attention! I clicked on it and went to a church website in Essex, England. There I found a reference to the rosary, its history and confirmation from the New Testament as to Our Lady's age.

---

[22] A decade is the name given to each group of ten beads. [Eds.]

So what? Any of the searches could have told me that, but as this particular site had drawn my immediate attention I clicked on the history tab and found this:

Our Lady Queen of Peace, Braintree, Essex, UK,

A community of Franciscan Sisters in 1897 bought Bridge House, which belonged to Madame Edith Arendrup neé Courtauld the widow of Col. S.T. Arendrup. Edith, who had been converted to the Catholic faith on her marriage in 1873, was pleased to sell this white house with 5 adjacent cottages to the nuns. At first, the sisters used one of the large rooms as the Chapel, but when this became overfull the studio in Convent Lane was used. Soon permission was given to extend Bridge House and to include a Chapel. Sir John Francis Bentley, architect of Westminster Cathedral, designed the new Chapel and the foundation stone was laid on 26th March 1898 by Dean Lucas - with great difficulty according to the records owing to the very bad weather, with rain and gales. The Chapel was completed and opened on 25th May 1899.

This Chapel by the permission of the Mother Abbess, served for the next forty years as the Parish Church with a succession of chaplains, many from different orders. As early as 1897, French clergy of The Missionaries of Mary Immaculate were appointed to the chaplaincy. After the departure of the French priest in 1898, the Franciscan Fathers came from Stratford and, as there were four Priests, this enabled the holding of four Masses each Sunday. [23]

Four Franciscans from Stratford were helping to found a church. So I now had one more church for my growing list of

---

[23] This passage is no longer locatable on the internet, and so it is not possible to identify the site, or acknowledge the source of this quotation. [Eds.]

churches established by the Gorton friars. The Gorton Franciscans including Bro. Patrick founded Gorton, Killarney, Stratford, Glasgow, Forest Gate, Chilworth and now here was another one. They were undoubtedly Gorton friars, who founded Stratford, and then Braintree. Unbelievable? No, absolutely incredible and beyond belief. Why beyond belief? Why did that website catch my eye above the others?

The Catholic Parish of Braintree was where I had been baptised. Whilst I was reading their website, my Mum rang on my mobile. When she had finished what she had to say, I asked where I had been baptised in Braintree. 'Our Lady Queen of Peace' was her reply.

The Courtauld family mentioned above were rich textile industrialists. I was born in the Courtaulds 'Cottage Hospital', founded by them, and baptised in this church, which was founded by friars from Gorton via Stratford.

Many times over the years I have told the story of Gorton Monastery, and the strange way that things had been returned or new information found; and many people have commented that perhaps I was born to find this story. Well baptism in a Franciscan church founded by friars from Gorton would give me the right credentials.

Return of the Madonna

A beautiful hand-painted statue of the Madonna and Child was one of many treasures that went from the Monastery during its years of neglect.

College lecturer Paul Rhodes, who died suddenly in 2005 from a heart attack at the age of 49, innocently bought the Madonna for less than £200 from an antique shop in Levenshulme about 10 years ago.

He had displayed it on the landing of his Mossley home and, when friends Christopher and Steph Beaumont arrived to clear the house, they didn't know what to do with it.

Only when Paul's parents, Gladys and Frank, from Dukinfield, mentioned the statue to their carpet cleaner, did they become aware of a possible link with the Monastery.

He told the couple that it sounded like the figure that had gone from there, and after looking up the Gorton Monastery on the internet, Steph rang me and told me the story of the statue. I selected some pictures showing various Madonna statues in the Monastery and went to Uppermill, where the statue was stored, to examine it.

I was astonished when I saw the statue for the first time because, up until then, I had been looking at black and white photographs. The sheer vibrancy of the colours on the statue took my breath away. I confirmed the statue was one of the missing treasures. Paul's parents then gave permission for the 4ft 5in plaster of Paris figure, which once stood in the Monastery's private chapel, to be returned. They had been thinking of giving it to another church, but then their carpet cleaner spoke up and the statue had been correctly identified.

Steph told me that "Everybody is delighted it is going back to the Monastery. Paul's mum used to sing opera and once sang there."

Chapter 15: Let there be light!

Return of the Cross

On the 26th October 2006, the crucifix designed by Fr. Cuthbert returned to Gorton Monastery. The crucifix, which measured 12 feet by 17 ft and weighed about 350kg, had been located at Pat Wengraf Ltd., an art dealer in London.[24]

---

[24] The crucifix had been sold at the same Sotheby's auction in which the twelve statues of Franciscan saints were supposed to be included. However, because it could not be proved that it was part of Pugin's original design for the church, and thus covered by its Listing, it was not possible to have it withdrawn from the sale. [Eds.]

The crucifix was being bought by a church in Florida for an estimated £70,000. All parties agreed that, whilst the crucifix was no longer legally owned by the Monastery, morally it belonged here. Patricia Wengraf kindly agreed to let the Trust have the crucifix back at the greatly reduced price of £20,000, reflecting the costs she had incurred in its purchase and restoration.

A decision was made to put the crucifix back in place early in the restoration, to take advantage of the scaffolding in place to restore the leaded glass windows around the chancel.

The scaffolding would give easy access to the three bars that supported the crucifix and still hung from the chancel arch. The three bars can be seen in the previous photograph.[25]

---

[25] The bars appear only very faintly in the picture on p130. They are clearer in the photo on p135. [Eds.]

The crucifix came back to Gorton fixed to an 'A frame' on the back of a low loader. When the frame was lifted from the low loader, it soon became clear that it was too wide to fit through the church doors. One side of the frame was removed, and the remaining frame holding the cross was then able to be carried into the church. There followed an astonishing sight as twelve men were involved in the operation to carry the cross, and were being watched by a woman in tears; Kath North who had come to witness the event. I still get goose bumps when I remember the symbolism of that sight. More was to follow as I took photographs of the cross's journey into the gloomy interior of the church, the shrouded body of Christ surrounded by the carriers whose high visibility jackets glowed in the dark.

Once the cross was safely on the ground at the top of the nave, the Foreman inspected the fittings on the cross and then inspected the bars hanging from the chancel arch. He shook his head and announced there were some 'bits of metal' missing from each of the three bars, and he would have to make some more to complete the job. Magic words! Some 'bits of metal.' I had heard those words before.

We used to work from a house to the rear of the Monastery, so as to be close to the building to show people around. People used to visit us and often brought mementos, photographs and items associated with the Monastery. One day Frank Rhodes, local historian and Friend of Gorton Monastery brought us a carrier bag with some bits of metal in it. He had been given these by the owner of an antiques shop in Droylsden. They had apparently come from the Monastery, and had been stored in the shop owner's garage for 11 years.[26] Daft as it may seem, we put them in the bath! The house was used as an office, not a home, and therefore the bath was never used. We had limited storage space, so the bath was an ideal choice.

We moved from the house in November 2005 to The Angels, a nearby school we had renovated into a community centre. I rang Audrey Bradshaw, the Trust administrator, to ask if we still had the bag with the bits of metal and she said they were in a cupboard. I went to fetch them, returned to the Monastery, and gave them to the foreman. He climbed back up the scaffolding and, within minutes, had assembled the bits of metal on the bars. Everything necessary to complete the job had been sat in the bath for many years, nobody knowing what on earth they were for. It is an amazing tale but one that was

---

[26] The Trust is indebted to John Murphy and Michael Johnson for carefully preserving these fittings. As will be seen from the following, the correct positioning of the crucifix proved to be the key which unlocked many of Tony's subsequent discoveries.

hugely significant, although we didn't realise it at the time. The significance was that the cross was now hanging exactly where it should be, and that proved to be vitally important.

Sir Brother Sun,
Who is the day and through whom you give us light.

On Midsummer's Day 2007, we were preparing for our opening event, a Midsummer's Night Feast, aimed at the business community to promote the Monastery as a corporate venue. It was a beautiful sunny day and, around lunchtime, I noticed that the lights from the two lancet windows at the south of the Church were falling on the nave floor in perfectly parallel lines, and also that the lights were as far down the nave as possible, due to the sun being so high in the sky. I thought no more about it until the end of September, when I noticed the same lights again falling on the nave floor in parallel lines but this time half way down the nave. Obviously, with the sun now lower in the sky, it was able to shine much further into the Church. What was interesting was that in three months the lights had travelled half the length of the Church. This made me curious as to how far the lights would reach into the Church during the next three months.

By November, the lights had reached the chancel and by December they were beginning to shine on the reredos either side of the altar. Throughout December the lights continued to shine higher and higher on the reredos, as the midday sun rose lower in the sky. By midwinter's day, there were two vertical columns of light shining on the reredos. An amazing sight but midwinter's day has no relevance in the Catholic faith. Christmas Day, however, is extremely relevant and so I decided to see what would happen on Christmas Eve (assuming that whatever might be visible on Christmas Day would also be visible on the Eve.)

My colleagues and I gathered in the Church around midday, and waited until the two lights moved across the reredos until they were shining on the reredos in vertical columns either side of the altar, seemingly standing on the chancel floor.

An absolutely astonishing sight but nothing compared to what lay in store. Because it was Christmas, we had all brought food to share and we went to the Friar's Pantry for our Christmas 'do'.

Over an hour later, I went back into the Church to see what was happening and was greeted by an astonishing sight. Whilst we had been gone, the sun had continued travelling west and sinking lower in the sky, and therefore the light from the windows had continued travelling across the altar from left to right and was shining even higher on the reredos. I witnessed a single column of light seeming to rise out of the altar and soar high up to illuminate the body of Christ on the crucifix, exactly to the crown of thorns.

If we had not had the 'bits of metal' and been able to put the crucifix back in its exact position, we might not have witnessed it illuminated so perfectly, or even worse, if we had not found the crucifix we would never have witnessed this event at all.

If you notice in the photograph the right hand light is now shining on the chancel arch. If you play back the sequence to before we witnessed the two columns centred on the altar, earlier in the day the right hand light would have also illuminated the body of Christ. I checked the following Christmas, and it does.

So on Christmas day, as the lights track across the chancel, the first one illuminates the body of Christ symbolising his birth; then there is a period of darkness in between, symbolising the passion of Christ on the cross; then the second light illuminates the body of Christ, symbolising the Resurrection. The story of Christ's life told in lights on Christmas Day?

I have absolutely no proof of that. We have no surviving architectural drawings and nothing recorded about the architect, Edward Pugin, using lights in this way. The accuracy of the clerestory lights illuminating the statues of the saints, and for anything like the crucifix being illuminated in such a way anywhere near Christmas is, however, pushing the bounds of coincidence too far.

Our Lady of Light

Also, I have seen another church designed by Edward Pugin where he is using light to illuminate features. On the visit to Ireland in 2005, when I had unwittingly driven through Bro. Patrick's birthplace, I had lunch with my Aunt Pattie and Uncle Jack. When I was talking about the Monastery, I mentioned Pugin and my aunt said that she thought he was the architect for her church. After lunch, we went to the Church of the Assumption at Lady Island. It is a quite beautiful setting and I immediately noticed that it had a north south alignment. The timing could not have been more perfect, for as we entered the church the light from the round clerestory windows was illuminating the round heads of Apostles adorning the clerestory walls.

So we are left with a hypothesis; Edward Pugin is using light to celebrate Catholic feast days and features in his churches. How can we test that hypothesis? Pick a feast day and see what happens! So I began to watch for any lights that might be significant. In June 2008, I noticed a white light with a gold border on the Lady Altar, caused by the setting sun. I watched over a few weeks as the light rose higher on the altar, moving diagonally upwards towards the niche that was occupied by a statue of Our Lady, which I have since discovered was Our Lady of Guadeloupe[27].

---

[27] Tony later changed his mind, because Our Lady of Guadeloupe is always depicted alone, and not holding the Christ Child. The statue instead incorporates references to two verses of scripture. Revelation 12, v1 describes a woman 'clothed with the sun and standing on the moon': this figure of Our Lady wore a gold robe, and She stands on a crescent moon. In Genesis 2 v15 there is a reference to Her Son 'crushing the serpent': the figure of the Christ Child held a cross, the base of which is crushing a serpent which is under Her feet. In July 2010 Graham North, photographer and long-time friend of the Monastery, spotted what he thought was a piece of copper pipe in the rubble behind the Lady altar. Tony later identified it as the wooden cross that had been held by the Christ Child, and it now stands in the place of the statue, on the ruined altar. The present whereabouts of the statue is unknown. [Eds.]

By my calculations the light would illuminate the statue sometime in mid August. A quick look on a Catholic Feast Day website showed August 15th to be the Feast of the Assumption when Our Lady's rise to Heaven, both body and soul, is celebrated. So there was the prediction suggested by my hypothesis.

I waited in the early evening of the 15th August and, as predicted, the niche that once contained Our Lady was illuminated in a white light with a gold border. Our Lady is depicted wearing a gold dress, and in that dazzling white light on the Feast of the Assumption she would have been an amazing sight.

And perhaps my favourite, as it was based only on my now certain conviction that Edward Pugin was deliberately using light to illuminate features in his churches and also because it involves St. Francis. I have a photograph showing a statue of St. Francis in the nave at Gorton, and I can identify its location in the nave at that time with reference to the Stations of the Cross. I have another photograph showing an identical statue but standing on the opposite side of the nave. The question was whether the Franciscans had two identical statues or were they moving the statue from side to side?

My guess was that the statue of St. Francis was on one side of the nave on the Feast of St. Francis, and during the day he would be moved to the other side as they celebrated his life. Why? So that he would be illuminated in the morning light and again in the evening light. The life and death of St. Francis celebrated in light on the Feast of St. Francis. The problem in putting this theory to the test was that, firstly, the next Feast of St. Francis was to be on a Saturday morning, and secondly, we no longer have the statue to be illuminated. The solution was my lovely friend and colleague, Alison Levesley, who above and beyond the call of duty, was persuaded to join me in the Monastery on a cold Saturday morning.

"What would you like me to do?" she said.

"Just stand over there and impersonate St. Francis", I replied.

So Alison waited patiently in the cold October morning, a modern day St. Francis, and as predicted, she was eventually bathed in a silver column of light where the statue of St. Francis originally stood. The following year (2009), it was my chance to stand where the statue of St. Francis stood but this time on the opposite side of the nave, and as predicted I was illuminated in a column of light. The life and death of St. Francis celebrated in light on his feast day.[28]

I am completely convinced that the architect is deliberately using light to celebrate Catholic feast days but I think it is at the request of the Franciscans.

---

[28] Tony later theorised that the statue stood on the left hand side of the church on October 3rd for the *Transitus* (the evening service marking the death of St. Francis) and was then moved overnight to the right-hand side, for the Feast of St. Francis on October 4th. [Eds.]

Over the past three years I have taken many pictures of the crucifix being lit by the morning and evening sun during the Easter period. For the first time, I managed to take a photograph actually on Easter Sunday morning and also on the Feast of the Ascension, both in the morning and in the evening. By placing a card where the tabernacle used to be, I also demonstrated that it would have been illuminated around noon on the Feast of the Ascension.

In writing this story I have gone back over all my photographs, and can demonstrate that from the earliest possible date for Easter, 22nd March, to the last possible day for the Ascension, the 3rd June, the crucifix will be lit by the sun in both morning and evening, as well as by sunlight striking significant parts of the altar. I have one photograph of the crucifix lit on the morning of the 4th March, which was slightly puzzling because it is outside the range in which Easter can fall. Because of the north south alignment of the church, however, it follows that if the crucifix is lit from at least 4th March to 3rd of June, then it will also be lit at least from 9^{tth} July through to 8th October. (The pattern of lights will be repeated after the midsummer solstice.) My prediction is that the sunlight will fall on the crucifix on the Feast of St. Francis on 4th October, and this intention is what causes the light to fall on the crucifix outside the range for Easter earlier in the year.

To continue the story of the architect using light to celebrate Catholic feast days, I think it is the Franciscans who briefed Edward about creating light at the Monastery. St. Francis composed the song 'Canticle of the Sun', in which he describes and gives thanks to Brother Sun, Sister Moon and Brother Fire.

Canticle of the Sun

Most high, all powerful, all good Lord! All
praise is yours, all glory, all honour, and all
blessing.

To you, alone, Most High, do they belong. No
mortal lips are worthy to pronounce your name.

*Be praised, my Lord, through all your creatures,
especially through my lord Brother Sun, who
brings the day; and you give light through him.
And he is beautiful and radiant in all his
splendour! Of you, Most High, he bears the
likeness.*

*Be praised, my Lord, through Sister Moon and the
stars; in the heavens you have made them,
precious and beautiful.*

*Be praised, my Lord, through Brothers Wind and
Air, and clouds and storms, and all the weather,
through which you give your creatures sustenance.*

*Be praised, My Lord, through Sister Water; she is
very useful, and humble, and precious, and pure.*

*Be praised, my Lord, through Brother Fire,
through whom you brighten the night. He is
beautiful and cheerful, and powerful and strong.*

*Be praised, my Lord, through our sister Mother
Earth, who feeds us and rules us, and produces
various fruits with coloured flowers and herbs.*

*Be praised, my Lord, through those who forgive
for love of you; through those who endure sickness
and trial. Happy those who endure in peace, for by
you, Most High, they will be crowned.*

*Be praised, my Lord, through our Sister Bodily
Death, from whose embrace no living person can
escape. Woe to those who die in mortal sin! Happy*

those she finds doing your most holy will. The
second death can do no harm to them.

Praise and bless my Lord, and give thanks, and
serve him with great humility.

*

In the second verse of the song, St. Francis describes Brother
Sun as having the likeness of Jesus Christ, his Lord. In life,
Francis could not bear to snuff out a candle and thereby
extinguish the life of his Brother Fire. On one occasion, his
habit caught fire and he forbids his brothers to put it out. The
frightened friars ran to fetch the Guardian, who to Francis'
regret extinguishes Brother Fire. Shortly before arriving in
Cornwall, Lady Trelawney renames the part of the estate given
to the Franciscans as 'Sclerder' and that is the Cornish and
Breton word for light. The small church she gives them is
called Our Lady of Light. It is because of these things that I
think it is the Franciscans who wish to celebrate through light.
The period of suppression of the Catholic faith in the British
Isles is known as the penal days and very often as the 'dark
penal days.'

The Franciscans on their modern day crusade are bringing
the 'light of St. Francis' back to our shores, to bring
illumination after the darkness and dark times of the penal
days. Not only did they build a church worthy of being the
headquarters of a modern day crusade, they built it in the
Divine Proportion. It may have a cathedral height but it doesn't
have a cathedral's length. The width of the nave multiplied by
the Divine Proportion gives us its height; and the height
multiplied by the Divine Proportion gives us its length. That,
together with the north south alignment, is the only way the
body of Christ on the crucifix could be lit on Christmas Day.

A painting of St. Francis by Patsy Allen

Would the Franciscans and Edward Pugin have known about the Divine Proportion? Almost certainly.

About 1496, Luca Pacioli, a Franciscan friar and leading mathematician, was invited to Milan to teach mathematics at the court of the Duke of Milan. In Milan, Pacioli met Leonardo da Vinci and they quickly became close friends. Mathematics and art were topics that they discussed at length, both gaining greatly from the other. At this time, Pacioli began work on the second of his two famous works, *Divina Proportione,* and the figures for the text were drawn by Leonardo da Vinci. Few mathematicians can have had a more talented illustrator for their book! The book, which Pacioli worked on during 1497, would eventually form the first of three books, which he published in 1509 under the title *Divina Proportione.* This was the first of the three books that finally made up this treatise, and it studied the 'Divine Proportion'. It contains the theorems of Euclid, which relate to this ratio. Clearly the interest of Leonardo da Vinci in this aesthetically satisfying ratio, both from a mathematical and artistic point of view, was an important influence on his work.

The Divine Proportion was also of importance in architectural design, and this topic was to form the second part of the treatise which Pacioli wrote later '....*it seems to me that the proper title for this treatise must be Divine Proportion. This is because there are very many similar attributes which I find in our proportion - all befitting God himself - which is the subject of our very useful discourse.*'[29]

'All befitting God himself' is the key to understanding Gorton Monastery. Did Edward Pugin really carry out hundreds of calculations to illuminate the crucifix and other significant features in the church or is it the Divine Proportion in action? Having used the Divine Proportion to set out the overall structure of the buildings, Edward also uses it to define the relationship of the individual parts of the building to each other and, in doing so, sets up the conditions that create such fabulous displays of light. Undoubtedly, the lights on the crucifix on Christmas Day are intentional, and are achieved by placing the crucifix at the right height and depth into the church. The same is true of the placing of the statue of Our

---

[29] Luca Pacioli (1509) *Divina Proprtione*, Paganius Paganinos:Venice.

Lady and St. Francis, though I'm not so sure about the crucifix being lit at other times.

I've just completed a calculation to work out what time the crucifix will be lit (if at all) on the Feast of St. Francis, using the date and time of the 4th March observation. Using Jodrell Bank's online astronomical almanac and the known longitude and latitude of Gorton Monastery, it is possible to find out the right ascension, declination, azimuth and elevation of the sun when the 4th March photograph was taken. Putting the same data back into the almanac, and setting the date to 4th October, the almanac gave a time of 10.34 a.m. Even with the online aid, it was a difficult computation to make. Having worked that out without the aid of a computer, Edward would then have to apply that knowledge to decide where and how high to put the clerestory windows to light the crucifix on each of the possible 74 days of Easter and Ascension.

My feeling is that a more likely explanation is that the Divine Proportion is at work. It is said that the Divine Proportion is at the heart of everything from the story of creation to the proportions of the human body and the movement of celestial bodies. Having created the 'divine' building and placed it in the right location, all Pugin has to do was sit back and let the cosmos, also in the Divine Proportion, take over. Just for a moment, imagine you are back in the days when it was believed that the earth was the centre of the universe and that everything else revolved around it. Also imagine that Gorton Monastery is the centre of that universe and as the sun 'revolves' around it on its divinely ordered path, it illuminates all parts of this divinely proportioned building.

Of course the sun does not revolve around the Monastery, but looking at it this way helps understand the celestial clockwork that Edward has created.

Could it be that Gorton Monastery is not just designed using the Divine Proportion but is a physical embodiment of the Divine Proportion? The Divine Proportion can be achieved in three ways; numerically, geometrically and algebraically. We've already seen the numerical way using the Fibonacci Series 0 1 1 2 3 5 8 13 etc.

Using geometry, we can create the Divine Proportion by creating a square with sides of 1, dividing the square into two then subtending an arc, using the centre point of the base of the square, from a top corner of the square down to the base line. The base line will now measure 1 (the original unit) and 0.618 giving an overall length of 1.61:

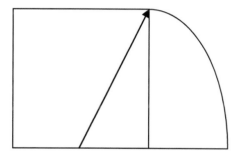

1 + 0.618

The third way of calculating the divine proportion is using algebra and the formula for this is:

Divine proportion = $\dfrac{1 + \sqrt{5}}{2}$

(One plus the square root of 5 divided by two) = 1.618

Now here is a strange thing. When I went looking for the proportion used to set out the chancel, and indeed found the proportions set out in the errors in the tiles, I didn't actually work out what the proportion was. In my excitement, I forgot my original quest. So, just to recap, I had established the proportion of the nave as the square root of 5 using Pythagoras' Theorem and in doing so had reduced the dimensions from 120ft x 60ft to 2 x 1. The dimensions of the chancel were 36ft x 48ft, and having deduced the classic 3 4 5 triangle, I hadn't carried out the calculation. So here it is:

$$X^2 = 36^2 + 48^2$$

$$X^2 = 1296 + 2304$$

$$X^2 = 3600$$

And, therefore, X is the square root of 3600, giving us 60ft. Now, in calculating the proportion of the nave, I had reduced the width of 60ft to 1, and we must do the same with the chancel, so the proportion in use on the chancel is: One. If you remember the beautiful little apse that is at the architectural heart of the building, it effectively bisects the building.

So how would we describe in words the architectural proportions of the building? Well it would be 'one plus the square root of five divided by two'. In other words, Gorton Monastery is the Divine Proportion!

Chapter 16: Joint Architect

From Fr. Justin we learn that, at the opening ceremony in 1872, a lunch was held afterwards at which 'the architect, Edward Welby Pugin, described Bro. Patrick not as Clerk of Works (which he had been magnificently) but as *joint architect*. He had worked with him for the past eight years, and he had reminded him of the friars of old.'

Great praise indeed but what exactly did he mean by *joint architect*? And where in the friary could over 250 sit down for lunch? I have often wondered over the years about this little mystery, and eventually the answer was revealed in 2006.

When the front wing of the friary was demolished in the 1980s, the exposed gable end was given a new brick skin. Because this was a modern intervention on a Grade 2* listed building, the modern bricks were removed in June 2006 during the restoration, and the crumbling plaster to the interior walls was stripped away. As the plaster was stripped back, an enormous bricked-up Gothic arch, nearly three quarters the height of the friary, was revealed. In addition, a smaller Gothic arch could be seen running at right angles to the larger one. Close examination showed that the arches had been free standing at some point, and only later had they been bricked up.

I knew from Frs. Agnellus' and Justin's histories, that the Franciscans had used St. Patrick's school to celebrate masses and that, when the first wing of the friary was completed, they used the library and dining room as a chapel, as the school was too small for the growing congregation. Fr. Agnellus showed a picture of the interior of the first school chapel in 'Assisi to Gorton' but, on closer examination, I could see that the picture was of a chapel inside the friary, the evidence of which we had just discovered.

Having completed the first wing of the friary, Bro. Patrick's need was for a chapel not a friary, as he and his Franciscan brothers were quite settled in Bankfield Cottage. So Bro. Patrick altered Pugin's design and turned the first wing of the friary into a church and, until 1872, this was used to meet the needs of the growing congregation.

Once the main church of St. Francis was completed, Bro. Patrick no longer needed the church in the friary, so he bricked up the gothic arches, put in new floors and converted it back into a friary.

Interior of the first Chapel in the Friary

Edward Pugin's remarks about *joint architect* all make perfect sense now, and the location of that opening ceremony lunch is now clear. The altar from the friary chapel was relocated to the new church, and the former chancel was used to house the 'top table' for the opening ceremony. The Minister General from Rome addressed the clergy; seated in what used to be the nave, from the chancel steps and from this same point, Edward Pugin also addressed the assembled clergy. I can imagine Edward stood there, both hands raised pointing to the chancel arch above him and making his *joint architect* remarks to the delighted pride of the Franciscans and amusement of the clergy. Bro. Patrick, a mere humble friar, had dared to alter Edward's masterpiece and to great effect.

Earlier I quoted Fr. Alexander Murphy saying he had witnessed Bro. Patrick at work and the following is his description of him at work in Glasgow.

155

In Labore Requies

(Thou art true rest in toil and sweat.)

'A stranger visiting a monastery is struck with the air of repose that pervades the entire place. That he has not reached a Sleepy Hollow is abundantly clear, for on all sides he finds wonderful activity. In lecture-room, library, workshops, laundry, kitchen, and garden, the Religious are busy with their allotted tasks; but their work is done in such a calm, self-possessed, and measured manner, that it intensifies the air of repose, which seemed at first sight to be due only to the quaint gables and the spacious cloister. He realises, perhaps for the first time in the life, that true rest may be enjoyed during the hardest toil. So should it ever be in the cloister. While the secular toiler seeks rest after his day's work is done, the Religious should so labour as to find it always. It is to be found through labouring in the presence of God, by the help of God, and for the glory of God. He who labours thus makes light of the usual forms of rest. It is the interior spirit, just adverted to, which distinguishes the Religious from the toilers outside, who, like himself, earn their bread by the sweat of their brow.

Many years ago the writer, when yet a youth in the world, witnessed a striking example of this. A squad of stonemasons were working around the recently laid foundations of a Franciscan church. All were clever workmen, and all were equally busy. But one of the number could be singled out as differing from the others, for his bearing suggested that he was resting in his work. All the while that he toiled and sweated his soul was in God's presence, and aspiration for God's help accompanied every stroke of the mallet, and the glory of God and the good of his Order were his sole ambitions. He was a Franciscan lay brother. Working in the open, in a Protestant city, his garb was that of the ordinary toiler, but his features

*reflected the restful spirit of a true Religious. He had found out
the secret, that if the toiler's mind and heart be with God, God
will be with him'*

Patrick Dalton, Glin

In December 2008, I went to Assisi and felt Bro. Patrick's
presence when I was in Chieso Nuova, a church built on the
site of the presumed birth place of St. Francis.

From that point on, I could hear the phrase 'Patrick Dalton
Glin' running through my head. Returning home to England,
the phrase kept on running through my mind and I woke in the
early hours of a Sunday morning and was unable to get back to
sleep, as all I could think of was 'Patrick Dalton Glin'.
Eventually I gave up on the idea of getting back to sleep and
logged on to my computer. I typed 'Patrick Dalton Glin' into a
search engine as I have done hundreds of times before and was
amazed to see the following result.

'A Short-Title Calendar of the Reception and Profession Books of...

*13: Same, 17 March 1878; First Order reception by Fr.
Arsenius Mertens of John Dalton, son of Daniel Dalton and
Maria Daly, born in Glin, (Limerick) in 1836 and named
Bro. Patrick*

Signed by same

*www.jstor.org/stable/30004546 - similar pages
by P.Conlan, 2000*

Clicking on the link only took me to the first page of the publication titled 'A short-title calendar of the reception and profession books of the English Franciscans in Killarney 1860-1902. Conlan, Patrick. 2000' but I was unable to view the entire transcription without a subscription to JSTOR – a scholastic resource site.

From what I could see, the entry was a record of Bro. Patrick's reception into the First Order and the names of his father and mother. I was a bit puzzled by the year of birth being given as 1836, when I had been working on the assumption that he was born in 1837.

When I went to work the following day, I logged onto the computer to show colleagues what I had found and typed in the magic words 'Patrick Dalton Glin' and found absolutely no searches matching the one I had found the previous morning. Even searching 'Patrick Dalton Glin jstor' produced no results, and to this day I have never been able to repeat that particular search result. Fortunately, I had copied and pasted the search result into an e-mail so still had the information. My friend and colleague Janet Wallwork was able to locate the publication, and arranged for me to see it. [30]

The following entries show Bro. Patrick's reception and profession into the Third and First Orders:

a) Reception of brothers for the English Friars

1: Anno Domini 1860 Die 2a mensis Novemberis in convent nostro Killarneyensi a Rvd Adm P. Archangelo Vendrickx, Ministro Provinciali, habitum tertii Ordinis receipt Joanees Dalton filius legitimus Danielis et Mariae

---

[30] The article was originally published in the journal *Collectanea Hibernica*, No 42 (2000), pp181-214. [Eds.]

Dalton, natus in Glin (Limerick) A.D. 1836, et vocatus est Fr. Patricus. In quorum fidem hoc una cum senior Discretorum signavimus Killerney hac 11a mensis Novemberis 1860 signed by Fr Patricus Verhestraeten, vicarious, Fr Eustachius Princen, Instructor.

Finally, nearly forty years later I discovered a use for the Latin lessons I'd endured at school! I remembered enough to be able to work out that John Dalton, son of Daniel and Maria Dalton, born in Glin (Limerick) in 1836, had received the habit of the Third Order from the Minister Provincial, Reverend Fr. Archangel Vendrickx on the 2nd November 1860 in Killarney, taken the religious name Patrick and had been received into the order by Fr. Patrick Verhestraeten on the 11th November 1860.

Behind those dry and dusty Latin words, there was a lot of information. Firstly, Bro. Patrick was the first person to be received into the Order and this was only months after the Franciscans had arrived in Killarney. Secondly, the fact that Bro. Patrick had received the Habit from the Provincial Minister of the Belgian Province suggests that this was a momentous occasion. And finally, details of his parents but still an uncertainty about the year of birth.

Having been received into the Order, Bro. Patrick would take his vows (be professed) a year and a day later, and the Profession of Brothers into the Third Order (again in Latin) shows him being professed into the Order on the 12th November 1861 in Killarney. Once again, the entry in the register gives the year of his birth as 1836 and Glin as his birthplace.

It was not until 1878 that Bro. Patrick enters the First Order. He was received into the First Order in Killarney on the 17th March 1878 (the Feast of St. Patrick) and, once again, we learn

159

that he was the son of Daniel Dalton and Maria Daly, and was born in Glin in 1836.

Bro. Patrick is professed into the First Order on the 19th March 1879, and we finally get some confirmation of his birth because the entry is quite specific. It says that on the 19th March 1879, there was a simple profession of Brother Patrick (John) Dalton, born in Glin on 7th October 1837. Into the hands of Fr. Arsenius Mertens; signed by Fr. Arsenius Martens, guardian, Edward Vercoustre and Bro. Patrick Dalton.

The full date of birth is given and this leads me to believe that it is correct, and certainly fits in with his age at death and the census returns. I have found no trace of Daniel Dalton and Maria Daly, as records for this period are conspicuous by their absence in Ireland. There are plenty of Daltons in and around Glin and there is at least one Daniel Dalton, a stonemason by trade, of the right age but at this time I have no way of telling if there is a connection.

So for now, the search for John Dalton who became Bro. Patrick has come to an end. At the time of writing this, 2009, it is the 100th anniversary of his death and the 800th anniversary of the founding of the Franciscans by that other builder of churches named John. Giovanni Bernadone, who as St Francis of Assisi, became known to millions around the world.

I think that Bro. Patrick would be mortified by the thought of this book, as by all accounts he was a very humble, pious man who got on doing what he did best; the building work. I think he would be the first to say "I'm just the builder. My Franciscan brothers are the men who are doing God's work." But in understanding what Brother Patrick was up to, we get a greater understanding of what his Franciscan colleagues are up to and, perhaps finally, the real answer to my initial question. Why on earth would you build a parish church of cathedral-like proportions, in farmland, to meet the needs of just 300 hundred Catholics scattered over 25 square miles?

This was never about a parish church. After over 300 years in exile facing persecution, imprisonment and bloody executions, the Franciscans are on a modern day Franciscan crusade. They build a headquarters worthy of a crusade and, from Gorton, Bro. Patrick goes out with a priest and builds a church and friary. The priest remains and Bro. Patrick returns to Gorton where he sets out with another priest to build a church and friary. Again the priest stays and Bro. Patrick returns to repeat the process.

In 1887, the Minister General, Bernadine a Fortogruaru, issued the Decree for the new Custody. The friaries at Manchester, Glasgow, Stratford and Killarney were separated from the Belgian Province of St. Joseph; and in February 1891 they were erected into a new Province. The Province of England of the Immaculate Conception had been created, all links with Belgian had been severed and Fr. David Fleming was made Provincial with Polycarp Vervoort as his Custos and Brendan Butti, Francis Verhagen, Aidan McCarthy and Cuthbert Wood as his Definitors. Fr. David chose Forest Gate as his headquarters and the balance of power shifted away from Gorton as the motherhouse. Slowly the memory of what happened here was forgotten, and the role of Gorton and its friars in the establishment of the Third English Province became lost in the mists of time. Through my journey following Bro. Patrick, the real story of Gorton Monastery has re-emerged. Gorton Monastery, not just a parish church but the headquarters of a modern day Franciscan crusade.

Another carved head

In 2007 our photographer, Graham North, took advantage of a skyhoist, which was on site to inspect the roof, to take high level photographs of aspects of the church's architecture. He even managed to get above the steeple to take photographs down onto it! When he returned to earth, Graham asked if I knew about a carved head high up on the church. As you can imagine, I am very familiar with all of the church's features but I was unaware of any carved head up there. I had once discovered a delightful carving of a monkey, which I am certain is one of Bro. Patrick's little jokes. I have this mental image of him striding about Gorton in his quest for bricks, with a raggle taggle of little Gortonians behind him chanting monkey, monkey, monkey in reference to his attire. And later, when he was busy at work carving stone, the little Gortonians would be delighted to watch as a little monkey gently emerged from the stone that Bro. Patrick was chipping away at.

Having looked at the photographs and gone to look at the carving on the label stop of one of the clerestory windows, there was undoubtedly a head carved up there. I knew it was the custom for the head mason to be allowed to put a carving of himself on the church, but most chose to carve someone else's likeness, and sometimes unflattering carvings of someone who had annoyed them in the course of the building works.

My first thought was that it was Edward Pugin because of the wavy hair, before a colleague quickly pointed out the carving was of a woman. I even remember his words, 'Idiot, it's a woman!' Of course it was but I had been too wrapped in the world of friars and priests to consider a woman. So whose head had Bro. Patrick carved on the church? Was it a childhood sweetheart? An unfulfilled love and the reason he entered the order? But then with absolute certainty the answer came to me – his mother.

The eyes are closed on the carving, which is symbolic of the person having died and the head is turned very slightly to the right. I had just returned from a holiday in France, during which I had visited the hauntingly beautiful American Cemetery above Omaha beach. I remembered reading that the graves are laid out in the traditional east to west orientation but that the headstones were turned slightly to face America, the land of their birth.

The head carved here at Gorton was facing Glin in County Limerick, Ireland.

A final and fitting thought is that Bro. Patrick was born on the 7th October 1837, and therefore he would have been Saturday's child and as we all know;

'Saturday's child works hard for a living'
Brother Patrick Dalton
7th October 1837 – 11th June 1909

Seanchaidhe: a Gaelic word for Storyteller

Many people have asked me if I work here at the Monastery, meaning am I paid or a volunteer. I laughingly reply 'No I play here' and in truth that is how it feels. For me, it has been an incredible journey of discovery and spirituality, that's not to say there haven't been hard times, but fortunately the good outweigh the bad.

Brought up as a Roman Catholic, I left my faith in the church behind as I moved into my twenties. My belief in God and Jesus Christ remained but was never particularly at the front of my mind. I did, however, question that from time to time, particularly in response to terrible tragedies like the unspeakably evil people at loose in the world causing death and misery to innocent people. When someone dies, we are told it is God's Will and for those dying before their time, we are told they have gone to a better place. I distinctly remember the lowest point of my faith as the terrible heart rending images of the Indonesian Tsunami filled the news at Christmas 2004. How could there be an all seeing, all powerful, all merciful God who could allow such terrible things to happen? Why didn't he take the murderers, child killers, terrorists and genocidal dictators and create a better place here on Earth? Why was it always the poor, the young and the innocent?

By this time, I was working full time at the Monastery and my colleagues were often talking of healing energies, Angels and other 'spiritual' matters; probably best described by the term New Age Spirituality. Over the years, I have met many wonderful people here at the Monastery who are proud of their Christianity, either expressed through traditional church worship or through aspects of New Age Spirituality. Whilst some of those beliefs were outside of my comfort zone, it was interesting to be able to discuss and explore them. I certainly wasn't in a position to criticise anybody's faith, as I had no faith or beliefs of my own. Looking back, I can now see how my journey here has not just been one of discovery but of a spiritual reawakening.

The search for Bro. Patrick and his brothers has meant that I had to understand what it was that inspired them and enabled them to produce such an incredible masterpiece here. The source of their strength and faith lies in their 'little brother' St. Francis and, through him, their devotion to Jesus Christ, God and the Holy Spirit. In researching St. Francis, I came to understand their love of him and to rediscover my faith in Jesus. It wasn't a road to Damascus experience; there were no trumpets and fanfares or heavens opening. I remember one day looking up at the crucifix and just accepting Jesus into my heart – it was as simple as that.

In discussing aspects of faith I often joked that 'I don't do spiritual, show me the evidence and I'll believe it'. My friend Alison used to introduce me as the 'channeling historian' meaning that I was getting my information or inspiration from the spirit world. I make no such claim but I am fascinated by the way in which this story was 'given' to me. I could have called this story 'A Comedy of Errors', as each new find was nearly always based on an error or an intuitive feeling. I have learnt not to ignore those odd feelings or coincidences, as they have always produced the evidence I sought.

The story is not over yet but it is time to have set it down. Thousands have people have enjoyed elements of this story on the guided tour programme I run at the Monastery. It is a fascinating story and, because it is one I believe in and happened to me, I can deliver it with great passion, so much so that tears are not uncommon. This used to bother me but friends have assured me that if I am reaching out to the hearts and minds of people, I should not alter anything. I love telling this story and, in doing so, it connects me on a deeper level with many of the audience and talk afterwards is often on matters of faith and spirituality. There is so much in religion that we can share, but sadly we identify ourselves by our differences not by the overwhelming amount we have in common.

So, in a sense, I have become *Seanchaidhe* or storyteller, which is a good Irish tradition. My parents are Irish, and in fact my father, like Bro. Patrick, was a Limerick man. If I had followed my mother's side of the family, like my grandfather and uncle perhaps, I would have become a lighthouse keeper, like them.

Now I think about it, perhaps I have.